GIRLS' WORLD

Making Cool Stuff
for Your Room,
Your Friends
& You

Joanne O'Sullivan

LARK BOOKS

A Division of Sterling Publishing Co., Inc.
New York

Library of Congress Cataloging-in-Publication Data

Art Director: DANA MARGARET IRWIN
Assistant Art Director: HANNES CHAREN
Cover Design: BARBARA ZARETSKY
Photography: SANDRA STAMBAUGH
Illustrations: ORRIN LUNDGREN
Editorial Assistance:
ANNE WOLFF HOLLYFIELD,
RAIN NEWCOMB

Published by Lark Books, a division of
Sterling Publishing Co., Inc.
387 Park Avenue South, New York, N.Y. 10016

© 2002, Lark Books

Distributed in Canada by Sterling Publishing,
c/o Canadian Manda Group, One Atlantic Ave., Suite 105
Toronto, Ontario, Canada M6K 3E7

Distributed in the U.K. by:
Guild of Master Craftsman Publications Ltd.
Castle Place, 166 High Street Lewes East Sussex, England BN7 1XU
Tel: (+ 44) 1273 477374 Fax: (+ 44) 1273 478606
Email: pubs@thegmcgroup.com, Web: www.gmcpublications.com

Distributed in Australia by Capricorn Link (Australia) Pty Ltd., P.O. Box 704
Windsor, NSW 2756 Australia

CONTENTS

Welcome to Girls' World!

The fact that you are reading this book right now tells me three really cool things about you!

1) You are *so* over watching endless re-runs on TV and playing video games.

2) You're *not* into spending all your money on stuff that looks just like the stuff every-body else has.

3) You are a completely original, creative dynamo bubbling over with imagination and ideas!

Yes, I'm talking about you!

You may think that only the kids who are good in art class are creative. Not true! Each of us is a totally unique person who can create in our own totally unique way. You don't have to be good at drawing or painting to be a creative person. You just have to have a good imagination, a can-do attitude, the right tools and materials, and of course, a little inspiration. That's what this book is here for!

Girls' World will give you new ideas and show you the way to bring your own cre-ative flair to every part of your life, from your bedroom to your birthday party. We'll tell you the stuff you need to get started and where you can find it, then give you step-by-step instructions on how to make your own incredible creations. You'll learn easy ways to change a simple ho-hum thing like a pen into an expression of personal style! You'll get great ideas for making the cool things you see in magazines, but yours will have more personality and cost less money. You can make just about anything you can buy, but making it yourself will be twice as much fun!

Creativity doesn't happen in just one place. It's something you bring to every part of your life. Once you've discovered it, it's there for good. Get excited about making things now, and before you know it, you'll be making your own clothes. Who knows, one day maybe you'll even design your own house!

Life will always be fun if you look at the world creatively. You'll always be able to find something to do when others are bored. You'll always be able to turn something ordinary into something special.

There's nothing like the feeling of finishing a project, taking a proud look at what you've made, and saying, "Hey! I made that!!" Give it a try! Use your imagination. Use your hands. Use your creativity, and make your world the way you want it to be.

Your World!
~.~.~.~.~.~.~.~.~.~.~.

Girls' World is divided into four sections representing the four most important parts of a girl's life:

In the HOME section, you'll find projects that will inspire you to look at your room, your own little corner of the world, in a new way. From making a fabulous flower curtain for your door to painting and stamping your sheets, there are a million different little ways to add personality and style to your room. Well, we only tell you about 20 different ways, but you'll come up with a bunch more ideas on your own!

In the SCHOOL section, you'll find projects that bring a creative spark into your school day. You'll learn to decorate your notebook covers, make fantastic pens, embellish your backpack, and even make your locker into a stylish place to stop between classes. We still haven't come up with any good ways to make your homework disappear, but we're working on it.

In the FRIENDS section, you'll find tons of ideas for making presents for your friends, and some great projects to make *with* your friends at parties and sleepovers. You can make beauty products right there in your kitchen, and jewelry and dream pillows, too. There are also some great gifts to make for your pets to show them they're special!

In the YOU section, it's all about you! You'll find projects and ideas for making your own jewelry, accessories, and bags. You'll learn cool ways to dress up T-shirts and even flip-flops. You'll never be able to look at a plain hair elastic the same way again because you'll have so many great new ideas for snazzing them up!

But can I *really* make all this stuff? you ask. Yes! You can! To help you, there are pictures of each finished project, instructions, and sometimes illustrations to give you a little extra visual guidance. The pictures are there to give you inspiration, the instructions are there to help you get there, but you'll bring your own creative input to everything you make.

How to Use This Book
~.~.~.~.~.~.~.~.~.~.~.~

You may feel like doing all the projects in the *Home* section by the end of the weekend, or you may just want to do one (that's probably more realistic). Look through the book and find the projects that really make you say "I wanna make that!," and go for it!

Sometimes when you're all excited about a project, you want it done NOW! Creativity doesn't work that way! It's a process, which means you need a little patience to get the result you want.

Take your time—this isn't a test—and enjoy yourself. Improvise. Try blue instead of pink, or vinyl instead of fake fur. Use beads instead of ribbon, or rose instead of lavender. Don't get frustrated or discouraged if your project doesn't look exactly like the one in the picture. It's OK. Even if your project flops, that's OK too. You're learning, and the next thing you make will be better.

Not every project is for everybody. Some are easy, some harder, and some you may have to work up to. To help you decide how hard something might be, we've devised a difficulty rating scale.

RATING SCALE

Do-It-Yourself Dabbler: Beginner level. This is easy, easy, easy. Even if you've never seen a hot glue gun before, you should be able to pull this one off.

Do-It-Yourself Diva: Intermediate level. You're ready for more of a challenge. Go for it!

Craft Queen: Advanced level. This project is for the brave, the bold, and the skilled. You may need to get a parent to help, too.

You may be a Dabbler now, but you can become a Queen in no time, with some patience and practice!

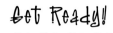

Get Ready!

Creative inspiration can strike you at any time. Be prepared to let your imagination carry you away! Have supplies on hand so you can go with your creative flow. Some girls are lucky enough to have a rec room or play room where they can keep their craft supplies. For the rest of us, there's a craft supply box kept under the bed, in the closet, or on top of the desk. Start a stash of supplies wherever you can.

Before you go shopping for craft materials, take a little tour of the drawers and closets in your house. A lot of the best stuff that you could ever find is sure to be right there in your own house. Look for safety pins, fabric scraps, costume jewelry, and old magazines to use for your projects. They'll come in handy for something, someday, so store them away.

Now that you've combed through your house, you'll have to head out to shop for the rest of the things you'll need.

Craft stores are a good place to start for your basic supplies. Where else can you find a hot glue gun, the ultimate craft tool? If you can't find something, or don't know what the material you want looks like, always ask a salesperson. They probably know exactly what you're looking for and where you can find it.

Yard sales and thrift stores are also great for those unique one-of-a-kind little decorations that make a difference in your projects. Did I mention that they're also very cheap?

Don't overlook the home improvement store—they have all kinds of cool stuff there. Tag along with your parents, and while they're shopping for gardening equip-

ment, scoot off to the paint aisles or even the specialty fastener area. Use your imagination, and you'll be able to make jewelry and tons of other items from materials you find there.

You could spend hours in fabric stores and not see all the great stuff there. Don't just look for fabric—spend time in the trim and notions sections. You can find all kinds of buttons, appliqués, foam, and cord to help you put together something special.

Finally, head to your local health food store. While your mom buys organic vegetables, you can be in the health and beauty section finding essential oils and other good natural ingredients for making natural beauty products.

When you shop for your materials, make different lists for different stores so that you won't have to make a lot of trips. Wherever you go, keep an eye out for materials. If it's cheap, cool, and interesting, get it—you'll find something to do with it later.

Materials and Tools
~.~.~.~.~.~.~.~.~.~

OK, so now you know where to go, but what exactly do you need? Well, you don't need all of the things on the following list, but if you were to put together a Craft Queen Starter Kit, these things would be in it. It's a good idea to buy items as you need them for projects that you're *definitely* going to do. When you're finished, save the leftover stuff. Before you know it, you'll have quite a collection of materials, and you won't need to go out and buy anything when the urge to make a new lampshade hits you.

glue, craft glue, glue sticks, wood glue)
Holograph paper
Hook-and-loop fastener tape
Magnet sheets or rolls
Nail polish
Paint (acrylic paint, dimensional paint, spray
    paint and glitter spray paint, paint pens)
Permanent markers
Polymer clay
Ribbon
Rubber stamps and stamp pads
Sequins
Silk flowers
Stickers
Synthetic turf
Clear tape
Wax paper
Beading wire
Yarn

CRAFT QUEEN STARTER KIT

TOOLS

Ruler
Tape measure
Scissors
Craft knife
Hot glue gun (and glue sticks)
Paintbrushes
Hole punch
Ruler
Measuring tape (a cloth one is useful)

DECORATING MATERIALS

Beads (seed beads, bugle beads,
    E beads, etc.)
Craft foam
Decoupage medium
Fabric scraps
Fake fur
Feather boas
Feathers
Felt
Flat marbles
Foam filler (for pillows)
Fringe (beaded or yarn)
Glue (fabric glue, glitter glue, epoxy, tacky

SEWING MATERIALS

Needles (see page 12 for more info)
Thread
Straight pins

BEAUTY PRODUCT MATERIALS

Sweet almond oil
Beeswax
Cocoa butter
Essential oils

Where Do I Get It?

As you look at the list of supplies for each project in this book, you may see this little symbol 🐷 next to an item. At the end of the list you'll see the symbol again, showing where you should be able to find the item.

Special Instructions

Every project in *Girls' World* is different. So, unlike a book that's just about knitting or beading, you're going to learn a lot of different techniques for making things. There are a few techniques that you'll be using for several different projects, so we thought we'd give you some general information about them so you can be prepared.

POLYMER CLAY BASICS

Working with polymer clay is fun and easy. You've probably worked with it before, but here are a few things you need to know if you haven't.

Polymer clay comes in two forms: in solid blocks that come in solid colors, and in "canes," which are long, round tubes with patterns inside them.

The tools you use when you work with polymer clay (knife, glass dish, rolling pin, etc.) shouldn't be used for anything else. Don't use Mom's best casserole dish or favorite rolling pin. You can get what you need at yard sales and thrift stores.

Wash your hands well with soap and warm water after you work with polymer clay.

Really well. Pay special attention to your nails—the clay tends to get under them when you work with it.

Always get an adult's permission to bake the clay in the oven (or toaster oven).

Read the manufacturer's instructions for correct oven temperatures and recommended baking times.

SEWING BASICS

When you see a beautiful purse or skirt that someone has made by hand, you may feel overwhelmed and think, "I could *never* do that!" But you can! Sewing isn't as hard as it seems, and like all things, it just requires dedication and practice.

Here are some basics to get you started:

THREADING A NEEDLE

Make a knot at one end of the thread so it won't come undone.

RUNNING STITCH

1. Bring your needle up through the fabric and back down again close to the first stitch.

2. Poke your needle back down through the fabric beside the place where it came up. Keep bringing the needle up and back down. Make the spaces even between your stitches. Stitch on top of your last stitch twice before you cut your thread.

BACKSTITCH

1. Bring your needle up from the underside of the fabric. **2.** Come back up again as you did for the running stitch, but poke the tip of the needle into the fabric at the end of the first stitch. Bring the needle out again in front of the thread, pulling it through.

3. Stitch on top of your last stitch a few times before you cut your thread.

Be sure to choose the right sewing needle for your project. There are two main kinds: *sharps* are long and thin, with a small eye used for regular thread; *darners* are thick, have a big eye, and are used with yarn and embroidery floss. If you're making something that needs to be really sturdy (such as the Blue Jeans Forever Bag on page 103), you'll need embroidery floss and a darner. For more delicate projects (such as the Dream Pillows on pages 79-80), you can use a sharp and regular thread. Try to choose thread that will blend with the material you're using.

Craft CAUTION!!

Burns, cuts, pin pricks, and singed hair. Do we have to suffer to create? Not if we use common sense, exercise a little caution, and above all ASK FOR HELP!! Anything that involves heat, cooking elements, or sharp objects can be dangerous. Of course, you've got common sense and you wouldn't do anything silly like climbing a stepladder by yourself, but for all those *other* people who might, this is a reminder to use caution.

When you see this symbol next to a project, it means you're going to need an adult around while you do this project.

HOT GLUE GUN SAFETY

Picture this: You're just getting really into your project. You get a little carried away, forget that your glue gun is BURNING hot, you touch it, and OUCH! It hurts, and your burn mark doesn't look so great either. There are tons of projects in this book that involve using a hot glue gun, so remember to follow these guidelines.

✿ Always read the instructions *first*!

✿ Always use your hot glue gun on a flat surface. They usually come with a stand to keep them upright. Don't lay your hot glue gun down, or something could catch fire.

✿ Keep your fingers away from the tip.

✿ Don't touch the glued spot until it cools down.

✿ ALWAYS unplug your hot glue gun when you're finished using it!

SCISSORS AND CRAFT KNIVES CAUTION

Since you like to make things, you're probably pretty comfortable with scissors and craft knives. That doesn't mean you should be reckless! If you're working too quickly and your hand is in the way, you could really hurt yourself. When working with anything sharp, go slowly. Keep your hands out of the path of the scissors or craft knife. When you're finished with your project, put your scissors or craft knife away so you won't get hurt and no one else will either.

HOT STUFF

To make some of the natural beauty products in the book, as well as anything involving polymer clay, you've got to use a stove or an oven. Wait until there's an adult around to try one of these projects. Turning on the oven may seem like a simple thing to do, but when you're dealing with gas and electricity, you never know what could happen. Be on the safe side and let an adult turn cooking appliances on for you.

FUME-Y ROOMS

If you're painting, or using epoxy or super strong glue, work outside where there's plenty of fresh air. Fumes from paint and strong glue can be very dangerous. Plus, they really smell bad! If you can't work outside because it just happens to be winter or you live in Antarctica, open some windows in the room where you're working. You should open a window if you're working with nail polish for a long time, too. If you're cold, just put on a sweater! And don't forget to shut the window when you're done with your project.

Now Can We Start?

We've talked about the thrills, prepared for the dangers, now the adventure begins—let's start creating!

13

Home

There's no place like home!

THERE'S NO BETTER PLACE TO EXPRESS WHO YOU ARE THAN RIGHT THERE IN YOUR VERY OWN ROOM.

You do your homework there, hang with friends, and do your best thinking and dreaming there. Put your own personal style stamp on it!

Take a good look around your room. What do you like? What do you want to change? You don't have to make big changes or spend a lot of money to get a new look. Small changes can have a big impact. Move something around. Add a little something. Turn an ordinary thing into something special, something YOU!

In this section of the book, you'll learn to make projects that let you apply your creativity to everything from your mirror to your bulletin board. Even little things like a lampshade or a curtain can reflect your style. Imagine what you could do with a big thing like your bed!

Changing your surroundings will change the way you look at things. You'll enjoy the time you spend in your room, and your creative energy will flow. Reimagine your room and get busy on your redo! Today your room, tomorrow the world!

Ooo La Lampshades

OK, SO MAYBE YOUR PARENTS WON'T LET YOU PAINT A DOLPHIN MURAL ON YOUR BEDROOM WALL, OR COVER YOUR HEADBOARD IN SYNTHETIC TURF. DON'T WORRY. START WITH SMALL CHANGES TO YOUR DECORATING SCHEME. A LAMPSHADE IS A PERFECT PLACE TO ADD SOME FLAIR TO YOUR ROOM WITHOUT A LOT OF TIME, MONEY, OR FUSS. YOU'LL BE SURPRISED HOW MUCH PERSONALITY A COOL LAMPSHADE CAN ADD. THESE FOUR STYLES CAN MATCH ANY DECOR AND ARE SO EASY TO MAKE. COVER YOUR SHADE IN SILK BUTTERFLIES, MAKE A COOL BEADED FRINGE SHADE, A FABRIC-COVERED CLASSIC, OR A WOVEN WONDER.

Fly by Night Lampshade

Get Ready!
~.~.~.~.~.~.~.~

Blue acrylic paint

Paintbrush

Lampshade

A bunch of silk butterflies

Hot glue gun and glue sticks

1. Mix your paint with water to thin it out. This makes a "wash" that you can paint onto the lampshade. Paint it and let it dry for 1 hour.

2. Hot glue your butterflies to the lampshade. That's it!

Classy Lassie Lampshade

Get Ready!
~.~.~.~.~.~.~.~

Square lampshade

Big piece of craft paper

Pencil

Straight pins

Spray adhesive

Fabric

Beaded ribbon trim

Hot glue gun and glue sticks

1. First, make a paper pattern of the lampshade. Lay your lampshade down on its side (any side) on the craft paper. Trace along the top and bottom edges of the lampshade where the shade touches the paper. Now rotate the shade so that the next side of the shade is laying on the paper, and trace the edges touching the paper again. Keep doing this until you've traced all four sides of the shade on the craft paper. This will make a pattern of the shade on your paper. Cut out the pattern.

2. Place the paper pattern on the fabric and pin it in place. Cut out the fabric following the pattern.

3. Spray adhesive onto the lampshade and wrap the fabric around it (make sure there aren't any wrinkles!). You'll need to spray outside where there's plenty of fresh air to blow away the smell.

4. Hot glue the beaded trim to the lampshade.

Fringe Bins

Get Ready!
~.~.~.~.~.~.~.~

Lamp

Top ring of a lampshade 🐛

Thread ☞

Scissors

Ruler

Cardboard

Beads (lots of them!)

Clear nail polish (optional)

Polymer clay (optional)

🐛 *You can find top rings at lamp shops or you can buy (and take apart) an old shade you bought at a yard sale.*

☞ *We used nylon crochet cord. You can also use embroidery thread, yarn,* knotting cord, or hemp cord. The thicker the thread, the fewer threads you'll need for the shade. Try out different cords, and be sure you try your beads on the cord. There's nothing worse than really wanting those icy blue glass beads and finding out you can't slip them on that heavy cord you chose!

1. Select your top ring. Here's a way to find out if your top ring will look good on your lamp: Drape a length of thread or cord over the ring. Does the thread touch the lamp base anywhere or does it hang freely? If the thread touches the lamp, use a larger ring.

2. Unwind and cut off about 3 feet (91 cm) of thread. Fold it in half.

3. Hang the folded thread over the top ring. Bring the two loose ends through the loop. Pull the ends to tighten the knot (see Figure 1). Decide how long your fringe will be, then add ½ inch (1.3 cm) before you trim the thread.

4. Remove your thread from the ring and lay it out on a table. Measure it with a ruler.

5. Measure and cut a piece of cardboard as long as your thread and about 6 inches (15.2 cm) wide. At one narrow end, make a cut in the cardboard about 1 inch (2.5 cm) deep.

6. Slip the end of your thread into the cut. Wind your thread around and around the long piece of cardboard. Keep winding. You'll need a lot of thread.

7. Slide your scissors under the thread at one end, and cut the thread. Fold these threads in half and cut them again the same way.

8. Thread several beads onto a single length of thread. Seven or nine is a good number to use. Tie a simple knot at the very end of the thread. Repeat the process, threading beads onto all the threads and knotting the ends.

9. Follow the directions in step 3 for tying the thread to the ring. Be patient. Keep threading and tying. Vary the number of beads you have on each end.

10. If your thread ends begin to unravel (or you find it hard to slide beads on the thread), dip the

thread end in clear nail polish. Let it dry and then slide the beads on.

11. When you have completed your fringe, you may need to use the scissors to neaten the ends.

FIGURE 1

17

Finally, a Finial!

You can transform a drab metal finial (the thing that you screw on the top to hold the shade) into a funky finial with a little polymer clay. Read the directions for working with polymer clay on page 11. Simply make a large clay shape in colors to accent your fringe shade, push the finial into the clay, and bake it. Voila, you're done!

Tickled Pink Lampshade

Get Ready!

Cylindrical lampshade with straight sides

Measuring tape

Ruler (optional)

Calculator (if you can't divide)

4 spools of ribbon of equal width in different colors

Scissors

Hot glue gun and glue sticks (optional)

Craft glue

1. Use a measuring tape to find the circumference of your shade (the circumference is the measurement around a circle). Wrap the measuring tape around the shade tightly. Write down the measurement.

2. Now it's math time. Use the ruler to measure the width of your ribbon. Divide the circumference of your shade by the width of your ribbon. If your shade's circumference is 28 inches (71.1 cm) and your ribbon is 1 inch (2.5 cm) wide, you'll need 28 lengths of ribbon. If your answer is, say, 16.34, then use 16 ribbons. You can space them as needed.

3. Measure the height of your shade. Write down the measurement. Add 1 inch (2.5 cm) to this measurement, then measure and cut the number of ribbons you needed in step 2. Set the ribbons aside.

4. Lay the lengths of ribbon over the top ring of the shade in the color pattern of your choice. Space

them evenly. When you like how the ribbons are spaced, glue one end of the ribbon just over the metal ring. You can use a hot glue gun and glue sticks or craft glue. Let the bottom of the ribbon hang free for now.

5. How tall was your shade? Divide the height of your shade by the width of your ribbon. If you didn't follow directions and write down the measurement, you'll have to measure all over again! The answer you get will tell you how many lengths of ribbon you'll need for weaving. Write down the answer. Remember, if your answer is 14.75, then use 14 ribbons.

6. Measure and cut a length of ribbon equal to your ribbon measurement in step 1, plus ½ inch (1.3 cm) just to be on the safe side. Measure and cut as many pieces as you found you would need in step 5.

7. Start weaving the ribbons around the shade. Start at the top of your shade. Weave the ribbon over and under until you get to where you started. Trim the ends with scissors, and glue them down.

8. When you have finished weaving, wrap the end of each vertical ribbon just over the bottom ring. Trim them if you need to, and glue each end to the inside of the shade.

What Would Your Ideal Bedroom Look Like?

Everything would be purple. I don't care what the fabric would be or what the other decorations are as long as they're purple.
YESENIA LEVETTE MORALES 10
New London, CT

I would have a day bed and it would be decorated with purple and silver. The mood would be East Indian!
ANDREA ESPERENZA MACIAS, 13
Phoenix, AZ

In my ideal room, I would have my own movie theater, tons of animals, popcorn and cotton candy machines, a canopy bed, lickable wallpaper that tastes like chocolate, and a remote control that when you press a name on a button your friend would appear right in front of you.
STEFANI ARIZA, 9
Plantation, FL

Wherever I lay my hat, that's my home.

19

Friendship Tree Photo Holder

SO MANY FRIENDS, SO LITTLE SPACE FOR THEIR PICTURES ON YOUR DRESSER. LOOKING FOR A SOLUTION? DISPLAY ALL YOUR FRIENDS' PICTURES AT ONCE ON A SPARKLY PHOTO HOLDER. EACH WIRE IS LIKE A BRANCH ON A TREE, BLOOMING WITH A BEAUTIFUL PICTURE OF YOUR FRIEND. YOU CAN EASILY PUT IN A NEW PICTURE WHENEVER YOU HAVE A NEW FRIEND TO ADD TO THE BUNCH OR WHEN AN OLD FRIEND GIVES YOU A MORE RECENT PHOTO.

GET READY!
~.~.~.~.~.~.~.~

Polyfoam dome

Sequins

Sequin pins

1 piece of wire for each photo ☛

Scissors (or wire cutters)

1 hair clip for each photo

Craft glue

craft stores

☛ *We used floral wire (the stuff they use to tie bouquets together at a flower shop).*

1. Cover the entire surface of the polyfoam dome with sequins. Just poke a sequin pin through the middle of each sequin and stick it into the dome.

2. Use the scissors or wire cutters to cut the wire into different lengths—if all the lengths are the same size you won't be able to see all the photos because they'll overlap. You may need to experiment a little. If your wire is too tall, the photo holder may become top-heavy and tip over.

3. Push one wire up through the opening near the spring at the back of a hair clip. If the wire doesn't fit into the opening, you can wrap it around the clip. Add a drop of glue where the wire and clip spring meet to make sure it stays in place.

4. Poke the wires (with the hair clips now attached) into the dome between the sequins. Make sure the tallest wires are located at the back of your photo holder.

5. Open each hair clip and insert a photo of a friend! Bend the wires and rearrange them if you need to so that you can get the photos to look the way you want them to (you can take out the wires, cut them, and put them back in if you need to).

Switch Hits!

REMEMBER: WHEN REDOING YOUR ROOM, START SMALL, VERY SMALL. THERE AREN'T TOO MANY THINGS IN YOUR ROOM SMALLER THAN THE LIGHT SWITCH COVERS—YOU KNOW, THOSE LITTLE PLASTIC THINGS THAT GO OVER YOUR ON-OFF SWITCH. USUALLY THEY'RE BORING BEIGE, BUT THERE'S NO REASON YOU CAN'T TURN THEM INTO FASHION STATEMENTS. DO THEM UP WITH COLLAGE OR GLITTER, OR COVER THEM IN CLAY—IT'S A GREAT WAY TO ADD SOME PERSONALITY TO YOUR WALLS WITHOUT PAINTING THEM.

Collage Covers

GET READY!

New, clear plastic light switch cover ✿

Pencil

Scrap paper

Magazines

Scissors

Glue stick

Wax paper

Screwdriver

✿ *home improvement stores*

1. Take the light switch cover apart. There's a paper template inside. Lay the template on a piece of paper and trace around it, including the hole for the switch. You'll want to work on more than one collage, so make several traced templates.

2. Cut out the traced templates (including the hole for the switch).

3. Flip through your magazines. Look for something that catches your eye for the background of your col-

lage, such as a flowery-patterned dress or the shiny metallic paper in a car advertisement. Spread some glue on the template and press on the paper you found. Turn the paper over, trim the edges, and cut out the switch hole.

4. Now comes the really fun part. Light switch covers with themes are easy to do. Find the things in magazines that really interest you: lips, eyes, patterns, skateboards, shoes, words—you name it. Rip out a lot of pages and make a stack of them. Sort through the stack and cut out the things you really like. Play around with putting them in different positions on the background before you glue them on. When you're happy with the way they look, glue them down. Slip your collage into a folded sheet of wax paper and press it under a heavy book overnight.

5. Get an adult to unscrew your old light switch cover and put on your new one.

Seeing Spots Light Switch Cover

GET READY!
~·~·~·~·~·~·~

Regular light switch cover

Polymer clay (in two different colors)

Rolling pin

½-inch (1.3 cm) round cookie cutter

Small sharp knife

1. Roll out a large flat sheet of polymer clay. The clay should be thin, like a piece of bologna. Place it on the light switch cover and press down around the edges. Cut off the excess. Trim out the hole for the light switch.

2. Roll out a large flat sheet of polymer clay in another color. Cut out dots with the cookie cutter. Press the dots onto the light switch cover in a random design.

3. Bake in a toaster oven at 275°F (135°C) for 10 minutes.

Glittery Covers

GET READY!
~·~·~·~·~·~·~

Regular light switch cover

Clear plastic light switch or outlet cover 😈

TAKE YOUR PICK
~·~·~·~·~·~·~

Nail polish, clear and glitter

Big laser-cut glittery shapes

Glitter

Glitter glue

😈 *home improvement stores*

Paint a regular light switch cover with glitter nail polish. You'll need to give it three coats, letting each layer dry before painting on another. Do your last coat in clear nail polish to make sure it doesn't chip.

Try a glittering outlet cover, too. Take out the backing of a clear light switch cover and pour some laser-cut shapes on the inside. Squirt glitter glue over them. You may have to do a little rearranging to make sure the whole cover is coated. Let it dry overnight, then do touch-ups if necessary. Put the backing back on and you're done!

Stick 'Em Up Bulletin Board ◉

BORED WITH YOUR BULLETIN BOARD? GIVE IT A LITTLE PERSONALITY! GRAB SOME PAINTBRUSHES AND PAINT IN TONS OF COLORS, THEN DESIGN, DOODLE, AND DECORATE YOUR BORING BOARD. WHEN YOU'RE DONE, MAKE BOLD AND ONE-OF-A-KIND PINS, GATHER ALL YOUR COOL PHOTOS AND POSTCARDS, AND STICK 'EM UP!

GET READY!
~.~.~.~.~.~.~.~.~

Cork bulletin board with wooden frame

Masking tape

Newspaper

Acrylic paints

Small paintbrushes

TAKE YOUR PICK
~.~.~.~.~.~.~.~.~

Paint pens, gel pens, and dimensional paint

Small rubber stamps

1. Spread a layer of newspaper on the cork surface. Bring the edge of the newspaper right up to the edge of the frame and slide it underneath. This will keep paint from dripping onto the cork.

2. Tape off three or four areas of the frame. Paint

23

the areas different colors, and let them dry. Give them an additional coat if needed, then remove the tape when the paint is dry.

3. Tape off other areas of the frame and paint them. Lay the tape on previously painted areas to make neat edges for the next color. Continue taping and painting the frame until it's completely painted.

4. Use paint pens, gel pens, dimensional paint, or acrylic paint to create patterns on the solid colors. Dip the handle end of a small paintbrush into acrylic paint to make small dots. All you have to do is touch the handle to the surface and you'll have a perfect dot. Simple brush strokes going in different directions make an interesting pattern, too. Just keep adding patterns to the painted surface. Use gel pens to cover the surfaces with words you like or your friends' names. Use your imagination!

Polymer Pins

GET READY!

~.~.~.~.~.~.~.~

T-pins

Polymer clay in a variety of colors

Small clay cutters (optional)

Glass baking dish

1. First, read the general directions for polymer clay on page 11. Knead the clay until it is soft and warm.

2. Roll marble-sized balls of clay. Single colors are fun, but polka dots are even better. To make dotted balls, roll tiny balls of clay, put them on a larger ball, and then roll the ball. The tiny balls flatten out into dots.

Use opposite colors of balls on each side of the T if you wish. Press them onto the T part of the pins. Gently press them together.

3. Another option is to roll single-color coils of clay—they should be about the same thickness as a marking pen. You can also roll thinner coils in different colors and twist two coils together. Trim a short length of coil and press it onto the T-pins.

4. Place the pins on a glass baking dish, and bake them according to the manufacturer's instructions.

Happy is the house that shelters a friend.

Picture Perfect Frames

DON'T YOU LOVE GETTING YOUR PRINTS BACK FROM THE PHOTO DEVELOPER? YOU RUSH TO OPEN THE ENVELOPE, TAKE A LOOK AT ALL YOUR GREAT PICS, AND REMEMBER ALL THE FUN YOU HAD WITH YOUR FRIENDS OR FAMILY. DON'T LEAVE THOSE SNAPSHOTS SITTING AROUND IN A DRAWER! FRAME THEM UP SO YOU CAN ENJOY YOUR MEMORIES EVERY DAY. HERE ARE JUST A FEW IDEAS FOR MAKING FUN, FANTASTIC FRAMES.

Mega-Watt Sparkle Sequin Frame

GET READY!
~.~.~.~.~.~.~.~.~

Wooden picture frame

Pencil

Scrap paper

Sequin tape 🐾 in different colors, about 10 yards (9.1 m)

Plastic jewels

Hot glue gun and glue sticks

🐾 *fabric stores*

1. Trace the shape of your frame onto your scrap paper. Using the image as a guide, sketch your design and choose which colors of sequin tape will go where. You may even copy your sketch onto the frame with a pencil.

2. Once you've decided on the design, start cutting your sequin tape. Piece by piece, apply hot glue to one side of the sequin tape and press it in place on the frame. Add a little drop of hot glue to each end of the sequin tape to make sure the tape doesn't start to unravel and cause the sequins to fall off.

3. Hot glue the jewels in place according to your design.

4. Trim any excess sequin tape that may hang over the edges of the frame. Apply a dab of hot glue at the ends to seal the tape in place.

Dragonfly Frame ◉

GET READY!
~.~.~.~.~.~.~.~

Painted picture frame

Painted wooden dragonflies 🐾

Pearlized dimensional paint

Hot glue gun and glue sticks

🐾 craft stores

1. Paint a long swirling line on your frame with the dimensional paint. Allow it to dry.

2. Hot glue the wooden insects to the frame.

3. Slide your favorite picture into the frame and enjoy the view!

Dressed Up Drawer Pulls ◉

OK, NOW YOU KNOW HOW EASY IT IS TO GIVE YOUR ROOM A NEW LOOK BY CHANGING LITTLE THINGS HERE AND THERE. BUT WHAT ABOUT THE BIG THINGS, LIKE FURNITURE? EASY! YOU CAN UPDATE A DRESSER OR NIGHTSTAND WITH SOME FUN DRAWER PULLS. FLAT MARBLES BACKED WITH COOL PAPER ARE A GREAT SHORTCUT TO A NEW LOOK. THE PATTERNS YOU SEE ON THE PAPER ARE MAGNIFIED THROUGH THE GLASS. YOU CAN CHOOSE ALL MATCHING COLORS AND PATTERNS FOR YOUR DRAWERS, OR USE A DIFFERENT ONE ON EACH.

There's no place like home!

GET READY!

~·~·~·~·~·~·~·~

Ordinary round wooden or plastic drawer pulls

Screwdriver (optional)

Flat marbles

Electric hand-sander and sandpaper (optional)

Hot glue gun and glue sticks

Acrylic paint or nail polish

Small paintbrush

Scissors

TAKE YOUR PICK

~·~·~·~·~·~·~

Nail polish

Holographic or wrapping paper

Magazines

Craft glue (clear drying)

1. Remove your drawer pulls from your drawers. Usually you just have to twist them off. For some kinds, you'll need to unscrew with a screwdriver, starting from the inside of your drawer.

2. If your drawer pulls have a rounded face, you'll need to sand them a little to make the surface flatter. Better still, have one of your parents do it. Then repaint the pulls with acrylic paint or nail polish.

3. Decide what color combinations you want on your drawer pulls, and cut out pieces of holographic paper, wrapping paper, or patterns from magazines that feature your chosen colors. Cut the paper a little larger than a flat marble.

4. Glue the patterned side of the paper to the flat back side of the marbles. Let the glue dry for about 20 minutes, then trim the excess paper so there's none hanging over the edges of the marbles.

5. Hot glue each marble to the top of a drawer pull.

6. Screw your drawer pulls back into the drawers and admire your new dressy dresser or nightstand!

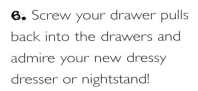

27

IMAGINE WALKING THROUGH A CASCADE OF FLOWERS EVERY TIME YOU ENTER YOUR BEDROOM! THIS FANTASTIC FLOWERED DOOR CURTAIN IS EASY TO MAKE AND WILL ADD A DRAMATIC TOUCH TO YOUR ROOM. YOU WON'T JUST WALK INTO THE ROOM—YOU'LL MAKE AN ENTRANCE!

Make an Entrance Door Curtain

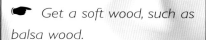

GET READY!
~.~.~.~.~.~.~.~

Spray paint

Wooden dowel (cut to the same size as your door frame) ☛

Measuring tape or ruler

Marker

Screw eyes

Clear plastic straws (about 30)

Scissors

12 pieces of fishing line, each 6-feet (1.8 m) long

Hot glue gun and glue sticks

Tiny silk flowers (about 200) ☛ ☛

Nails (optional)

Hammer (optional)

Masking tape (optional)

☛ *Get a soft wood, such as balsa wood.*

☛ ☛ *These came in bunches of about 20 in each color.*

1. Spray paint your dowel the color of your choice, and let it dry.

2. Mark equal spaces on your dowel and screw in your screw eyes. If your wood isn't soft enough to just screw them in, start a hole first with a nail and then screw them in.

3. Cut the straws into 2-inch (5.1 cm) pieces. Cut all the stems off the flowers.

4. Make a knot in one end of each piece of fishing line.

Put a big glob of hot glue on top of the knot. The glue glob will act as a stopper to keep the straws and flowers from falling off the fishing line.

5. String the flowers and the straws onto the fishing line, alternating straw, flower, straw, flower.

6. When you get to the end of the fishing line, tie it around the eye screw and make a knot. Repeat for each piece of fishing line.

7. Get a parent to secure the curtain to the top of the door frame with screws, nails, or masking tape.

NOTE: Instead of a dowel, you could use a sturdy piece of ribbon and sew your fishing line strands to the ribbon at equal intervals with a needle and thread. Then you could tack the curtain over your door with thumbtacks.

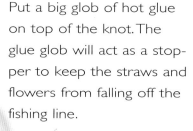

28

29

Superstar Mirror

MIRROR, MIRROR, ON THE WALL, WHO'S GOT THE COOLEST MIRROR OF ALL? YOU WILL WHEN YOU MAKE THIS ONE! THIS MIRROR IS THE PERFECT PLACE TO TRY OUT ALL YOUR NEW DANCE MOVES, PRACTICE SINGING INTO YOUR HAIRBRUSH, REHEARSE YOUR LINES, AND TRY ON THE OUTFIT YOU'LL BE WEARING TO THE MTV MUSIC AWARDS. A GIRL CAN DREAM, RIGHT? JUST BECAUSE IT LOOKS AWESOME DOESN'T MEAN IT'S HARD TO MAKE. GIVE IT A GO!

GET READY!
~.~.~.~.~.~.~.~

Full-length mirror

Yard stick

½ yard (45.7 cm) of fake fur ☛

Large piece of heavy-duty cardboard

Hot glue gun and glue sticks

Scissors

Craft knife

Sequin stars

☛ *Fabric comes in different widths. You'll need a 50-inch (127 cm) width for this fur.*

1. Measure and cut four 5-inch (12.7 cm) strips across the width of the fur. You'll now have four 5 x 50-inch (12.7 x 127 cm) strips of fur. Try to find which way the fur naturally falls, and cut in that direction. In other words, you want the fur to lay smooth rather than stick up, so smooth out your fur and cut toward the way the fur falls when smooth.

2. Measure the dimensions of your mirror's frame (not the inside part that touches the mirror, but the outside part). Add 4 inches (10.2 cm) to the length and width, and cut a piece of cardboard to this size.

3. Attach the cardboard to the back of the mirror with hot glue. Keep the mirror

centered on the cardboard so there is a 2-inch-wide (5.1 cm) border on each side all the way around.

4. Look at the frame of your mirror to see where the short and long pieces of the frame meet. You'll notice that the two pieces are cut with mitered corners (see illustration, above left). You'll want to cut your fur in this same manner. Measure the top width of your mirror and its cardboard border. Add 2 inches (5.1 cm) to that measurement, and cut your fur (with mitered corners) to fit this measurement. Start at the inside edge and wrap your fur around the back of the mirror, securing it in place with hot glue. Do the same for the bottom of the mirror.

5. Measure the long sides of your mirror the same way you did for the short sides. Cut the fabric and miter the corners in the same way, too. Wrap the excess fur around to the back of the cardboard and hot glue it down.

6. Attach the stars to the fur with a very small dab of hot glue (too much will melt the sequins).

30

senting—
e girl you've all been
waiting for... Jasmine!!!

mirror, mirror on the wall...who's the coolest of them all???

31

Hippie Chic Earring Hanger

HOW OFTEN HAS THIS HAPPENED TO YOU? YOU'RE GETTING DRESSED FOR SCHOOL IN THE MORNING, AND YOU'RE JUST ABOUT READY TO GO. YOU REACH FOR THAT FINISHING TOUCH FOR YOUR OUTFIT, THAT CUTE PAIR OF EARRINGS THAT YOU LOVE, WHEN AAAAGH! THERE'S ONLY ONE EARRING THERE! WHERE COULD THE OTHER ONE BE? DID THE DOG EAT IT? IS IT IN THE VACUUM CLEANER? LET THESE GROOVY GIRLS KEEP TRACK OF YOUR EARRINGS FOR YOU!

GET READY!
~.~.~.~.~.~.~

Precut craft foam shaped like groovy clothing

Picture frame with glass

Seed beads

Beading wire

Pliers or tweezers

Ruler

Scissors or wire cutters

Wire screen

Hot glue gun and glue sticks

1. Each girl has 10 strands of hair with 20 beads each. To make hair for each girl, take a 6-inch (15.2 cm) piece of beading wire and fold it in half. Thread 10 beads onto each half of the wire (starting at the end opposite the fold). Make a little loop at the end of each side of the wire by twisting the end of the wire back under the part that's beaded. Bead 10 wires in this way.

2. Divide the wires into two groups of five wires for each girl's hair. Bunch each group together and tie them in the center by twisting a small piece of wire around them.

3. Take the glass out of the frame. Measure the opening, and cut the screen to this size. Insert the screen. Push down the frame's metal tabs to keep it in place.

4. Now, hot glue the craft foam clothes and beaded hair to the frame. You're done!

WHAT'S THE WORD, GIRLS?
WHAT DO YOU WANT TO TELL
THE WORLD (OR JUST YOUR
LITTLE BROTHER) TODAY?
FEELING GOOD? DRAW A SMI-
LEY FACE. WANT YOUR SPACE?
TWO WORDS: KEEP OUT! YOU
CAN CHANGE YOUR MESSAGE
AS OFTEN AS YOU CHANGE
YOUR MIND.

GET READY!
~.~.~.~.~.~.~

Dry-erase board with
marker

Iron-on mini-dots

Iron

Feather boa

Strand of iridescent beads

Hot glue gun and glue
sticks

Fabric butterflies

Ribbon

CaN I TaKE a MESSaGE? BoaRD

1. Decide on a shape,
design, or permanent mes-
sage for your board and
use the iron-on dots to
attach the message to the
board (follow the manufacturer's instructions). We
made squiggly designs with
the dots.

2. Hot glue the feather
boa to the edge of the
message board.

3. Now it's time to attach
the iridescent beads to the
board. You can make loops
and swirls with the beads,
or just hot glue the strand
straight onto the board's
edge. When you've com-
pletely covered the edge,
cut the strand and hot glue
it to the board. Save the
leftover part of the strand
for later.

4. Hot glue the butterflies

to opposite corners of the
board.

5. Take the top off the marker. Hot glue your leftover
strand of beads to the marker cap. Hot glue the other
end of the strand to the back
of the message board. Hot
glue a piece of feather boa to
the cap. Cover the marker
base with the ribbon, twisting
the ribbon and securing it
with dots of hot glue.

33

Get Me My Agent! Phone

FINALLY—A PHONE OF YOUR OWN! NOW YOU CAN MAKE ALL YOUR SUPER-IMPORTANT, SUPER-PRIVATE CALLS (LIKE CALLING YOUR HOLLYWOOD AGENT ABOUT YOUR NEW MOVIE) BEHIND CLOSED DOORS IN YOUR OWN ROOM. IT'S ALL YOURS, SO DON'T HOLD BACK—DECORATE IT! USE ANY LEFTOVER PAINTS YOU HAVE FROM OTHER PROJECTS. WE LIKED THE SHIMMER AND SHINE OF NAIL POLISH, SO WE USED LOTS OF IT TO GIVE AN OLD PHONE A MAKEOVER!

GET READY!

~.~.~.~.~.~.~.~

Old phone

Pencil and scrap paper

TAKE YOUR PICK

~.~.~.~.~.~.~.~

Dimensional paint, acrylic paint, or paint pens

Nail polish (colored and clear) ☞

Nail polish remover (just in case)

☞ *You'll need several different kinds.*

1. First, unplug your phone! You'll just have to keep all your callers holding as you work on your masterpiece. Remember to avoid deco-

34

rating any part of the phone that has contact with electrical wires. Paint or nail polish drips inside could cause a short circuit, and then your phone would be history!

2. Trace the shape of the handset part of the phone (the part you speak into and listen from) onto paper so you can sketch your design for it first. For the base of the phone, you'll have more room to work with, so decide where you want to decorate, then be spontaneous!

3. To make perfect circles on your phone, here's a tip. Use a pencil to lightly trace around a coin. Outline the shape with paint or polish, then fill it in. You'll probably need two coats.

4. For tiny dots, dip your brush in nail polish and then lightly touch it to the surface. Don't press, just touch it. If you're using paints, use the tip of the handle to make small, perfect dots.

Easy Breezy Curtain

CAPTURE ALL THE COLORS OF THE RAINBOW AND HANG THEM RIGHT THERE IN YOUR WINDOW. A SPLASHY RIBBON CURTAIN IN THE WINDOW CAN BRIGHTEN UP EVEN THE DRABBEST ROOM AND LIFT YOUR SPIRITS ON A RAINY DAY. IF RAINBOW COLORS AREN'T FOR YOU, PICK RIBBONS THAT

MATCH YOUR ROOM'S DECOR: ALL ONE COLOR OR ALTERNATING STRIPES. YOU'LL DISCOVER THE BEST THING ABOUT THIS CURTAIN IF YOU'VE GOT YOUR WINDOW OPEN ON A BREEZY DAY— THE RIBBONS BLOW BACK AND FORTH IN THE WIND IN A BEAUTIFUL DANCE OF COLOR. ONE MORE IDEA: YOU COULD USE IT IN THE DOORWAY, TOO!

GET READY!
~.~.~.~.~.~.~

Tension curtain rod

Spray paint (optional)

Measuring tape or ruler

Grosgrain ribbons in various widths ☛

Scissors

Hot glue gun and glue sticks

☛ *Craft and fabric stores always have ribbon on sale. You can use any ribbon that is not wired on the edges. You'll need a lot of ribbon to make this project. Buy more than you think you'll need— you can always find something to do with the extra ribbon.*

1. Measure the width of your window or doorway. Get a tension rod that widens to at least that size. You can change the color of the rod from a plain white or gold to a bold color with a couple of coats of spray paint. Be sure you let the paint dry before you start hanging ribbons from it!

2. Measure the length from the top of your window to the windowsill. Add 2 inches (5.1 cm) to this measurement. Measure one ribbon to this length and cut it. Use that ribbon as a guide to cut the rest of your ribbons.

3. Wrap one end of the ribbon over the curtain rod and glue it to itself on the back side with hot glue. The ribbon should be close to, but not touching, the rod. Continue gluing each ribbon, leaving a little space between each. You can create a simple color pattern or mix up the colors and widths to match your mood.

4. Hang the curtain in the window. Use the scissors to trim the ribbon as needed.

Sweet Dreams Hand-Stamped and Painted Sheets

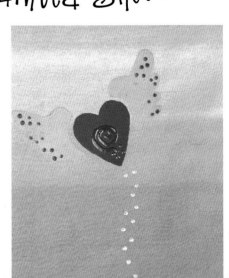

HAVING TROUBLE FINDING THE PERFECT SHEETS? LET'S TRY A LITTLE HYPNOSIS. YOU ARE GETTING SLEEPY, VERY SLEEPY. CLOSE YOUR EYES. IMAGINE YOUR BED. WHAT DO YOU SEE? WHAT'S THAT? HUNDREDS OF LITTLE FLYING HEARTS, SOARING AROUND IN THE CLOUDS, CARRYING YOU OFF INTO A DEEP AND RESTFUL SLEEP, FULL OF ROMANTIC DREAMS... OK, SNAP OUT OF IT AND OPEN YOUR EYES. YOU WEREN'T IN A TRANCE! YOU CAN MAKE THESE DREAMY SHEETS. IT'S SO EASY TO DO, YOU COULD MAKE THEM IN YOUR SLEEP (JUST KIDDING!).

Sheets and pillowcases in a light-colored pattern

Cardboard

Flying heart stamp

2 foam brushes, each 1 inch (2.5 cm) wide

Shader brush, size #4

Round brush, size #1

Fabric paint

Dimensional paint

1. Wash and dry your sheets.

2. Place a piece of cardboard inside your first pillowcase so the paint doesn't bleed through.

3. Apply paint to the stamp with the foam brushes. Paint the heart and the wings two different colors. Be careful not to put too much paint on the stamp or it will squeeze out the sides when you press down.

4. Carefully place the stamp where you want the image to be, and press firmly. It's OK if the design doesn't show up perfectly—you can fix it later.

5. Keep applying paint to the stamp and stamping the image until you've finished a pillowcase, then move on to the other pillowcase and the sheets.

6. Use the shader brush to fill in the hearts with more paint.

7. Use the round brush to fill in patchy spots on the wings. Allow the paint to dry.

8. To make small dots on the wings, spirals and zigzags on the hearts, and tails on the flying hearts, use dimensional paint.

9. Let the sheets dry flat for 24 hours before you use them, and 72 hours before you wash them.

37

AAAH! FINALLY, THE END OF THE DAY. YOU'VE GONE TO PRACTICE, DONE YOUR HOMEWORK, HAD DINNER...NOW IT'S TIME TO CHILL. WHERE CAN YOU GO TO GET SUPER-RELAXED AND HAVE SOME DOWNTIME? HOW 'BOUT CREATING A CHILL CORNER IN YOUR ROOM? IT COULD BE ANYWHERE—AN EMPTY CORNER, A WINDOW SEAT, INSIDE YOUR CLOSET (IF YOUR PARENTS WILL LET YOU TAKE THE DOORS OFF AND PUT IN A CURTAIN), OR ANY LITTLE NOOK YOU MIGHT BE ABLE TO FIND. YOU CAN MARK OFF YOUR SPACE WITH A FOLDING SCREEN OR HANG A DRAPE IN DREAMY FABRIC FROM THE CEILING—YOU WANT TO CREATE AN ENCLOSED AREA THAT SAYS THIS IS **YOUR** SPACE. GET A BUNCH OF OVERSIZE PILLOWS OR A BEANBAG CHAIR TO SIT ON. USE AN OLD TRUNK COVERED IN STICKERS OR A BED TRAY FOR A TABLE. KEEP A PORTABLE CD PLAYER AND SOME CDS AROUND FOR MOOD MUSIC, AND SCENTED CANDLES FOR AROMATHERAPY. STRING SOME MINILIGHTS OR ROPE LIGHTS AROUND FOR A COOL GLOW. ADD POSTERS AND PICTURES TO PERSONALIZE THE SPACE. A PERFECT ATMOSPHERE! NOW WHAT? WRITE IN YOUR JOURNAL, WRITE POETRY, OR DO DRAWINGS. FOLLOW YOUR CREATIVE MUSE (SEE STORY, PAGE 42) WHEREVER SHE LEADS YOU! IT'S YOUR TIME AND YOUR SPACE, SO RELAX AND ENJOY IT.

Home is where the heart is.

Make Your

A BED SKIRT HELPS PULL TOGETHER THE LOOK OF YOUR ROOM, AND LETS YOU USE THE SPACE UNDER YOUR BED AS AN EXTRA CLOSET. YOU CAN STOR YOUR STUFF OR EVEN HIDE YOUR MES UNTIL YOU HAVE A CHANCE TO CLEA UP (BUT DON'T TELL YOUR MOM I

Hula Girl Bed Skir

Looking for instant Hawaiian atmo phere and Polynesian perfection? Just get a few grass skirts at a part supply store, tie them together, and push the tops between your mat- tress and box springs. Trim the bot tom of the grass skirts if they're to long, or just push them further up under the mattress. That's it! Add some Hawaiian print pillows to your bed to match, or buy an inflatable palm tree to give your room a tiki touch!

Bed!!

TOLD YOU THAT). A FUN BED SKIRT CAN BE PART OF A BEDROOM THEME DECOR. OR, IF YOU DON'T WANT A THEME BEDROOM EVERY DAY, JUST USE THE SKIRTS WHEN YOU'RE HAVING A PARTY OR SLEEPOVER!

Party Girl Bed Skirt

Have you ever left a party wishing that it could go on forever? Well, with a bed skirt like this, the party never ends! Get a regular party table skirt (they're usually pretty long), and fit it to your bed as you did with the grass skirts.

This skirt looks really cool when it blows in the breeze of an open window or is tickled by the swirling current of a ceiling fan! Get some hot pink sheets or a purple comforter, and your bed will look like a float in a holiday parade!

CALLING ALL MUSES!

ARE YOU EXPERIENCING CREATIVE BLOCK? You know there's a great idea somewhere there in your head, but you just can't quite put your finger on it. So you sit, staring at the blank piece of paper, the uncut material, or the blob of clay, without a clue about what to do. Try calling a muse to help you out!

In Greek mythology, the Muses were nine sisters whose sole purpose in life was to inspire artists and help them to create. They were the daughters of Zeus (the king of the gods) and Mnemosyne (the goddess of memory). Each sister specialized in an art or area of study, and she would help humans who wanted to pursue her speciality. In ancient Greece, poets, actors, and storytellers would start their performances by asking their particular muse to help them do their best work. There were festivals and shrines to the muses, and schools named after them. In fact, the word *museum* comes from the word muse.

Nowadays, people use the word muse to describe anyone who inspires a person's creative urges. Photographers and designers often have a "muse" who they say is the source of all their inspiration. Some people are even inspired by their cats and dogs! Who or what is your muse? Try thinking about that person (or pet) and see if it helps your creativity. Or just close your eyes and clear your mind. Maybe one of the muses will pay you a visit.

Here are the nine muses and the arts they represent:

TERPSICHORE—DANCE

THALIA—COMEDY

CLIO—HISTORY

ERATO—LOVE POETRY

CALLIOPE—EPIC POETRY

EUTERPE—MUSIC

URANIA—ASTRONOMY

MELPOMENE—TRAGEDY (DRAMA)

POLYHYMINA—SACRED POETRY

ERPSICHORE

THALIA

CLIO

ERATO

CALLIOPE

EUTERPE

URANIA

MELPOMENE

POLYHYMINA

Mein haus ist dein haus.

Mi casa es su casa.

My house is your house.

There's an old saying "Happy is the house that shelters a friend." In cultures all over the world, sharing your home with a friend is one of the most important ways to show respect. Open your doors and welcome in a new friend! Above: Best friends Maggie and Marion visit each other's homes in Germany and the United States. Marion's house is seen above, and Maggie's house is the one below it.

43

Private Time Clock

SNOOPY LITTLE SISTERS ALWAYS TRYING TO READ YOUR DIARY? THIS CLOCK KEEPS TIME AND YOUR SECRETS SAFE, TOO. MAKING A CLOCK IS NOT AS HARD AS YOU MIGHT THINK. YOU CAN BUY A WHOLE SET-UP (CALLED A CLOCK MOVEMENT) AT HARDWARE OR CRAFT STORES. THE BODY OF THIS CLOCK IS JUST A CARDBOARD BOX COVERED IN CRAFT FOAM. WANT TO SEE TIME FLY? MAKE THIS PROJECT IN PRACTICALLY NO TIME!

GET READY!
~.~.~.~.~.~.~

Square cardboard box with a lid

Clock face template (see illustration, on page 45)

Pencil

Ruler

Nail or something sharp to poke a hole in the card-board lid

Clock movement

Craft foam sheets

Scissors

Safety pin

Fabric paint (regular and glow-in-the-dark)

Stickers

Beads

Craft glue

Batteries (see manufactur-er's specifications with clock movement)

🐱 *craft or hardware stores*

1. The top of your box lid will be your clock face. With your pencil and ruler, draw a big X from corner to corner on the top of the lid. The center point of the X is the center of your lid, and that's where you'll need to poke a hole for the shaft of the clock. Take a

look at the shaft to see how thick it is. The shaft will need to fit snugly inside the hole you poke. Make sure the nail or sharp object you use to poke the hole is about the same thickness as the shaft. If it's too big, the shaft will slip around in the hole. Once you're sure of the measure-ment, poke a hole in the center of the X.

2. Trace the bottom of your box onto the back of your craft foam sheet (the side without a pattern), then cut out the square and glue it to the box. To cover the sides of the box with foam, you'll need to put the lid on first. Cut your foam squares so that the top of the foam reaches the point where the lid ends. The width of the side pieces will vary slightly because of overlap. Cover two sides (across from, not touching each other) first, then complete the other two sides.

3. Cover the lid of the box in the same way. Cover the top first, then the sides. For the clock face, you'll need to poke a hole in the foam to match up with the hole in the box lid. Just turn the lid upside down so you can see the hole, then poke from the back to the front through the hole and through the foam.

4. Use the clock template (above right) and reduce or enlarge it on a photocopier until it's the right size for your box. You can trace it and tape your tracing to the lid, then poke small holes through the tracing paper with a safety pin at the

...plate as a guide to draw your own clock face freehand.

5. Insert the clock mechanism into the hole in the

box lid so the shaft pokes though the hole and the rest of the mechanism fits tight up against the inside of the box lid.

6. Use glow-in-the-dark fabric paint, stickers, and beads to make the numbers on the clock face. Just be sure not to attach any material that sticks up enough to get in the way of movement of the clock's hands when they're attached.

7. Once your decorations are in place and dry, attach clock hands following the manufacturer's directions.

8. Put the batteries into the back of the clock mechanism, hide whatever you like inside the box, and attach the lid.

Cyber Girls Computer Monitor Frame Cover

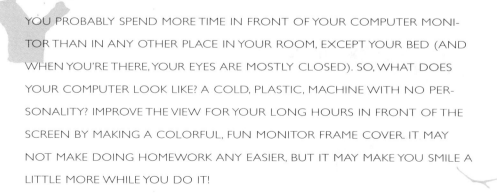

YOU PROBABLY SPEND MORE TIME IN FRONT OF YOUR COMPUTER MONITOR THAN IN ANY OTHER PLACE IN YOUR ROOM, EXCEPT YOUR BED (AND WHEN YOU'RE THERE, YOUR EYES ARE MOSTLY CLOSED). SO, WHAT DOES YOUR COMPUTER LOOK LIKE? A COLD, PLASTIC, MACHINE WITH NO PERSONALITY? IMPROVE THE VIEW FOR YOUR LONG HOURS IN FRONT OF THE SCREEN BY MAKING A COLORFUL, FUN MONITOR FRAME COVER. IT MAY NOT MAKE DOING HOMEWORK ANY EASIER, BUT IT MAY MAKE YOU SMILE A LITTLE MORE WHILE YOU DO IT!

GET READY!
~.~.~.~.~.~.~.~

Pencil

Ruler

Large piece of foam core

Craft knife

Foam filler or cotton batting
(optional) ☞

¼ yard (22.89 cm) of
vinyl

Scissors

Hot glue gun and glue sticks

Craft foam

Hook-and-loop fastener
tape in strips and dots

Rhinestones or plastic jewels

🐾 *art supply or office supply
stores*

☞ *You can buy this at fabric
stores. It's the stuff you put
inside pillows. Fabric stores
usually sell odd-shaped pieces
in bunches at bargain prices.*

1. Measure your computer
screen with a ruler, and
write down the measure-
ment. Next, measure the
frame around the screen.

2. Use your measurements
to draw the outline of your
monitor screen and frame
onto your piece of foam
core. Use a ruler so your
lines will be straight.

3. Add circles or free-form
shapes to the top and bottom outside corners of the
frame outline.

4. Run your craft knife
along the outside outline of
the monitor frame. You may
need to retrace along the
lines if your craft knife
doesn't cut all the way
through your foam core.
Once you've got your
outer frame cut out, trace
along the inner frame line,
cutting out the screen window. Keep retracing over
your lines if your craft knife
doesn't cut all the way
through.

5. Now you've got the
shape of the frame cut out.
If you want your frame to
be a little bit puffy, you can
cut foam filler or cotton
batting to fit the frame and
hot glue it to the foam
core.

6. Trace the shape of your
frame on the back of the
vinyl. Draw the outline of
the frame 1½ inches (3.8
cm) outside the frame you
just drew. Draw the outline
of the inner window frame
1 inch (2.5 cm) inside the
inner screen outline.

7. Cut the vinyl along the
outermost frame with a
pair of scissors. Next, cut
along your innermost
frame.

8. Slowly and gradually cut
at a diagonal from one corner of your innermost
frame so that the fabric
folds back a little. Fold the
fabric back and over the
adjacent corners of the
foam core frame. Pull the
fabric tight and start hot
gluing it to the back of the
frame.

9. Once you've got an
inner frame corner
attached, repeat the same
process with the outer corner on the same side. You
may need to trim the fabric
before you glue it down.
Just test out the placement
of your fabric by pulling it
tight over the back of the
frame and making sure that
it reaches and doesn't puck-
er. Repeat this process on
all four corners, starting
from the inner frame, and
then working to the outer
frame on the same side.
Keep on adjusting the fabric
and cutting and tucking as
needed until you've covered
the entire frame in vinyl.

47

10. Decorate the circles at the top and bottom corners of your frame. We made faces on the top two circles with plastic jewel eyes and mouths. Then we made removable craft foam hairdos for the cyber girls and attached them to the monitor frame with hook-and-loop tape. You could make multiple hairdos to change the look, or you could use hot glue for a permanent solution. We made flowers from craft foam for the bottom of the frame.

11. When you're happy with the look, attach the frame to your monitor with long strips of hook-and-loop tape. Attach the hook part to the back of your frame and the loop part to the monitor. You may want to hot glue the hook tape to the back of your frame for extra strength.

12. Attach the frame to the monitor, and enjoy the view as you work hard at your computer!

Fun Sun Catchers

SUN CATCHERS CAN ADD A NICE LITTLE SPARKLE TO YOUR WINDOW, LAMP, OR CEILING FAN. THEY'RE QUICK, EASY, AND CHEAP TO MAKE. A PAIR OF JEWELRY PLIERS IS HANDY TO HAVE AROUND, BUT THAT'S ABOUT ALL YOU NEED. CHOOSE THE PERFECT BEADS FOR YOUR CREATIONS, THEN SLIP THEM ONTO WIRE AND FORM THE SHAPES WITH YOUR FINGERS. IT'S LIKE SKETCHING WITH BEADED WIRE. THAT'S ALL THERE IS TO IT!

Soft, plastic-coated craft wire

Round-nosed jewelry pliers (helpful, but optional)

Toothpick or skewer

Pony beads (for the sun)

Bugle and seed beads (for the dragonfly)

Scissors

Monofilament

Dragonfly Sun Catcher

1. Cut off about 18 inches (45.7 cm) of wire. Make a small loop in the end.

2. Thread beads onto the wire, stopping when you've beaded about 2 inches (5.1 cm) of wire. Alternate bugles and seed beads. This makes the body of the dragonfly.

3. Thread on several seed beads and make a circle with the wire. Is it big enough for a head? If not, add some more beads. Wrap the end of the wire around the body to secure the head shape.

4. Use your tiniest and most colorful beads to make the wings. Thread about 2 inches (5.1 cm) of the wire with the beads, bend it back towards the body, and wrap the wire once around the body. Make another wing opposite the one you just made.

5. Make a second pair of wings right below the first pair. Wind the end of the wire tightly and trim it.

6. Shape the wings with your fingers.

El Sol Sun Catcher

1. Cut off about 18 inches (45.7 cm) of wire. Make a small loop at one end. If you don't have jewelry pliers, you can wrap the wire once around a toothpick or skewer to make a tiny loop.

2. Thread pony beads onto the wire. Alternate the colors if you are using more than one color. We used shades of yellow, orange, and red. You could use any combination of sunny colors. Leave a little bit of the wire's end unbeaded.

3. Lay the wire on a flat surface and wind it loosely into a spiral. Wind the end of the wire to the spiral.

4. Cut off about 24 inches (61 cm) of wire. Twist one end between two beads on the innermost part of the spiral.

5. Lay the spiral on a flat surface and wind the long wire around the next wire in the spiral. Continue winding until you reach the outermost part of the spiral.

6. Draw the rays of the sun with the wire. Make a triangle shape with the wire, wrap the wire around the outer part of the spiral between two beads, then make another triangle. Keep making triangles around the spiral until you get back where you started. Wrap the end of the wire tightly to the spiral and cut it off.

7. Cut off a length of monofilament, and knot the end to one of the sun's rays, so you can hang up the sun.

Special Collection CD Shelf

Who says girls aren't supposed to swing a hammer and pound nails? If you're careful and use some common sense, you can do almost anything. A trip to the local home improvement store will provide you with just about everything you need to build a one-of-a-kind storage shelf for your CD collection. Once you've learned to build a simple shelf, you may be inspired to build a bookcase, desk, or add an extra room to the house. There's no telling how far you'll go, girl!

GET READY!
~.~.~.~.~.~.~.~

¾ × 6-inch (1.9 × 15.2 cm) board (you'll need 2 lengths measuring 24 inches (61 cm) and 2 lengths measuring 6 inches (15.2 cm) 🐷

⅜ × 2 × 24-inch (9.5 mm × 5.1 × 61 cm) board

1 ¼-inch (3.2 cm) #16 wire brads ☞

Wood glue

Hammer

Drill and drill bits (optional)

Wood putty (to fill nail holes)

Sanding sponge or sandpaper

Spray paint (optional)

Acrylic paint

Masking tape

Small paintbrush

Rubber stamp and ink

🐱 Most home improvement stores carry a selection of "craft boards" or "shorts" sold in various lengths. You can have the lengths you need cut where you buy the lumber. We used three 24-inch (61 cm) boards for this project.

☞ These are very thin nails.

1. Get someone in the lumber section of your local home improvement store to cut the wood for you to the measurements on the list.

2. Work on a sturdy, flat surface. Stand the two 6-inch (15.2 cm) lengths of wood upright, then set a 24-inch (61 cm) length on top. Make sure the top

50

piece is even with the ends of the two standing pieces.

3. Take the long board off and set it flat on your work surface. Drive two nails partway into the board (not all the way through) at each end of the board.

4. Squeeze a thin line of wood glue onto the top of each of the two standing short pieces.

5. Carefully put the nailed board back on top of the standing boards. Even up the ends. Have an adult help you hold them in place. Gently tap each nail with the hammer until you feel it bite into the board. Don't whack too hard. Make sure your helper's hands are under the board, away from the hammer. When the pieces are secured and you can pick up the shelf without it falling apart, then you can hammer the nails all the way in. You can drive in a third nail at each end to make the shelf sturdier.

6. Turn the shelf over and repeat steps 2 through 5. Let the entire shelf set for an hour, and let the glue dry.

7. The finials will make the shelf legs. Hold one against the top board of the shelf. You can see where the screw hits the shelf. Move the finial around until you like how it looks. Press the screw end into the shelf to mark it. Mark the positions of the other finials.

8. Have an adult drill small starter holes for you, so you can screw in the finials more easily. Or you can just screw them in. Just before you finish attaching each finial, put a dab of wood glue under each one. Wipe off the excess glue if you used too much.

9. Use a nail to sink all of the nails. Just hold it on each nail and tap until it sinks a little bit below the surface. Put a little wood putty into the hole and let it dry.

10. Nail the 2-inch (5.1 cm) board to one side of your shelf. It will keep CDs

from sliding through the back.

11. Sand your shelf before you paint it. Use a spray paint or acrylic paint to paint your shelf. Spray paint is fast, but you have to cover the area around your shelf with lots of newspaper and work outside if you can. If you use acrylics, you'll only need a brush and something to cover the work surface. Whichever method you choose, give the shelf two or more coats. Let each coat dry before you put on additional coats.

12. Use short lengths of masking tape to make a checkerboard pattern on the front of the shelf. Paint in between the tape with a small brush, and let the paint dry. Remove the tape when the paint is dry. Paint the shelf legs if you wish.

13. You can make a more complex pattern if you use a rubber stamp in between each painted square or on every square!

51

School

HOW MANY HOURS A DAY DO YOU SPEND AT SCHOOL? SIX? SEVEN?

That's at least one-quarter of your day! School is a big part of your life, and while you're there you've got a lot to learn and do. You've got quizzes, tests, group projects, rehearsals, practices, and so many other demands in your busy school day. How can you find ways to bring creativity into your jam-packed schedule?

The projects in this section will show you how. You can make cool locker accessories, decorate your school supplies to make them one-of-a-kind, and even dress up your trusty old backpack. Study hard, have fun, and never miss a chance to use your imagination!

Turf Girl Notebook Covers

THERE'S SOMETHING ABOUT SYNTHETIC TURF THAT'S HARD TO RESIST. IT'S SHINY, IT HAS A COOL TEXTURE, AND UNLIKE REAL GRASS, IT LASTS FOREVER! A LITTLE TURF ON A NOTEBOOK COVER IS A FUN WAY TO MAKE A STYLE STATEMENT AT SCHOOL. ADD LOVABLE LADYBUGS AND DARLING DAISIES FOR A PICNIC RIGHT THERE ON YOUR NOTEBOOK COVER! NO WATERING REQUIRED!

GET READY!
~.~.~.~.~.~.~

Notebook with blank cover

Synthetic turf in the color of your choice 🐞

Pencil

Paintbrush

Craft glue

Scissors

Hot glue gun and glue sticks

TAKE YOUR PICK
~.~.~.~.~.~.~

Silk daisies

Plastic ladybugs and flowers

🐞 *home improvement stores*

1. Cut three rectangles of synthetic turf to fit on the front cover of your notebook.

2. Place the rectangles on the cover of the notebook, leaving approximately ¼ inch (6 mm) of space in between each. Mark along the outline of each rectangle with a pencil so you can put them back in the right place when you're ready to attach them.

3. Brush glue along the back side of one of the rectangles. Be sure to spread a solid layer of glue along each of the edges. Place the turf rectangle over one of the penciled outlines and press down firmly. Repeat with the other two rectangles. Let the cover dry for approximately 10 minutes.

4. Decide where you want to add the silk daisies or plastic flowers and ladybugs. Mark the spots on your turf. Apply hot glue to the back of your flowers and bugs, and press them in place. Let the glue set overnight to ensure that your decorations stay on even when you shove them into your overstuffed backpack.

Call of the Wild Binder Cover 🌀

THINGS CAN BE A LITTLE TAME AT SCHOOL. TAKE A WALK ON THE WILD SIDE WITH A COOL, FURRY BINDER COVER. PICK THE PRINT OF YOUR CHOICE—LEOPARD, ZEBRA, OR THE RAREST OF ALL FAKE ANIMAL PRINTS, BLUE CHEETAH! YOU'LL LOVE THE LOOK AND FEEL OF THE FABRIC—YOU JUST GLUE IT ON— AND YOU'LL LOVE ALL THE COMPLIMENTS YOU'LL GET!

GET READY!
~·~·~·~·~·~·~·~

Three-ring binder

Ruler

Scissors

Fake fur fabric

Craft glue

Craft brush

1. Open your binder out flat and measure the distance from cover to cover (that includes the front cover, the spine, and the back cover) and from top to bottom. Add 1 inch (2.5 cm) to the length and width of the measurement, and cut a piece of fake fur to that size.

2. Place your fur fabric, pattern side down, on a flat work surface, with one of the long sides facing you. Brush glue along the spine of the binder. Press the spine along the exact center of the fabric, leaving a ½-inch (1.3 cm) border of fabric along the top and bottom.

3. Now brush glue along one of the outside covers of the binder. While holding the binder closed, press the fabric to that cover (make sure to press it flat, and smooth out any folds or bumps). Repeat this step with the other cover.

4. Open the binder with the rings facing up. You will have a ½-inch (1.3 cm) border of fabric on all sides. Piece by piece, spread glue along the border, wrap it over the edge, and glue it inside the binder. You may need to cut some of the fabric around the ring part inside to make the fur fit well.

5. Measure the length and width of the inside cover of your binder. Subtract 1 inch (2.5 cm) from the length and width. Cut two pieces of fur fabric to this measurement.

6. Brush glue on the edges of the inside cover at the place where the overlapping fabric ends meet. Press down one of the pieces

you cut in step 4, making sure to line up the fabric so that you can't see the inside cover. Smooth out any folds or bumps. Repeat this step for the other inside cover.

Puffy, Poofy, Fun, and Floofy Pens ◎

IF YOU HAD BEEN BORN ABOUT 100 YEARS AGO, YOU WOULD HAVE BEEN WRITING WITH A REAL FEATHER (CALLED A QUILL) THAT YOU HAD TO DIP INTO A BOTTLE OF INK. VERY MESSY. THERE WAS ALSO ANOTHER PROBLEM WITH THAT SYSTEM. AT SCHOOL, EACH STUDENT HAD A BOTTLE OF INK ON HIS OR HER DESK. BOYS WOULD SIT BEHIND GIRLS, AND WHEN THE GIRLS BRUSHED THEIR HAIR BACK, BOYS WOULD GRAB IT AND DIP IT IN THEIR INK WELL. AREN'T YOU GLAD YOU LIVE IN THE 21ST CENTURY? YOU CAN STILL HAVE A COOL PEN THAT LOOKS LIKE A QUILL, BUT IT'S JUST A REGULAR OLD BALLPOINT PEN UNDERNEATH. AND YOU DON'T HAVE TO DEAL WITH ANNOYING BOYS!

55

Pens

Polymer clay

Plastic wrap

Feathers

Strand of mini-pearls

Toaster oven

Feather boa

Mini-marbles

Hot glue gun and glue sticks

Pink Pen

First, pop the ink cartridge out of the pen. Roll out a very thin sheet of pink polymer clay. Roll it around the pen and press lightly. Wrap the pen in a small piece of plastic wrap, and roll it gently on a hard surface to smooth the clay. Remove the plastic wrap. Cut off the excess clay from the top and bottom of the pen. Wrap the pearl strand around the top of the pen, pressing the pearls into the polymer clay. Bake the pen in a toaster oven at 275°F (135°C) for 10 minutes. Allow the pen to cool. Hot glue the feathers to the top end of the pen.

Blue Pen

Using blue polymer clay, follow the instructions for the pink pen up to the point where you cut the excess clay from the top and bottom of the pen. Then, make a thin snake of white polymer clay. Slice the white polymer clay into rice-sized pieces. Roll each piece into a small ball and press flat. Press the white pieces onto the pen randomly. Bake the pen in a toaster oven at 275°F (135°C) for 10 minutes. Allow the pen to cool. Hot glue small pieces of feather boa to the top end of the pen.

Blue and Purple Pen

Using purple polymer clay, follow the directions for the pink pen up to the point where you cut the excess clay from the top and bottom of the pen. Then, roll out a thin sheet of blue polymer clay. Trim it to ½ inch (1.3 cm) wide and roll it diagonally around the pen. Roll the pen in the mini-marbles, pressing firmly. Bake the pen in a toaster oven at 275° F (135°C) for 10 minutes. Allow the pen to cool. Hot glue the feather to the end of the pen.

Backpack Bug Zipper-Pull

NO, YOU CAN'T BRING YOUR PUPPY TO SCHOOL. OR YOUR CAT. OR EVEN YOUR GERBIL. HOW 'BOUT A LITTLE BEADED BUG TO KEEP YOU COMPANY? BEADING IS FUN, AND IT'S A GREAT SKILL TO LEARN. ONCE YOU'VE GOT THE BASICS DOWN, YOU CAN MAKE MORE AND MORE COMPLICATED FORMS. THIS LITTLE BUG ZIPPER PULL IS AN EASY BEADING PROJECT TO START WITH. USE THE SAME IDEA TO MAKE OTHER BEADED ANIMALS— YOU CAN BRING AS MANY OF THOSE TO SCHOOL AS YOU LIKE!

GET READY!
~.~.~.~.~.~.~.~

28-gauge silver-colored beading wire

22 #6 beads (body)

2 black #6 beads (eyes)

100 white or crystal #1 beads (wings)

Clasp

Silver crimp tube

Jewelry pliers

Scissors

 bead store

1. Measure and cut a 14-inch (35.6 cm) length of beading wire.

2. Bend the wire in half. Thread a single body bead onto one end of the wire; slide it up to the bend. Take the opposite wire end and slip it through the bead. Pull the two ends tightly to secure the bead.

3. Thread two body beads on one end of the wire. It doesn't matter which end.

4. Take the opposite wire and thread it through the two beads. Thread it in where the other wire comes out. Pull the two wire ends together to tighten.

5. Thread three body beads on one wire end.

Secure the beads just like you did in step 4.

6. Thread four body beads and secure them the same way you did in step 4.

7. Thread 20 wing beads on one wire. Thread 20 wing beads and two body beads on the opposite wire.

8. Thread the opposite wire through just the two body beads.

9. Squeeze the body beads together.

10. Add a row of two body beads. After you tighten the row, thread 30 wing beads on each wire.

11. Thread two body beads on one wire. Bring the opposite wire through the body beads and tighten.

12. Grasp a wing near the body and twist the wing. Be careful that you don't twist the end of the wire. Twist the other wing too. This will prevent your bug wings from spreading.

13. Make two more rows with two body beads in each row.

14. Thread one eye bead, then one body bead, and another eye bead. Tighten the row.

15. Place the two wires together and thread them through a crimp tube. Loop the wire over the bottom of the clasp and bring it back through the crimp tube. Use the pliers to crimp the tube. Trim off the ends of the wire as needed.

What's Your Favorite Thing about School?

I like art and gym class best. I also like to hang out with my friends.
BROOKE PACHINO, 10
Owings Mill, Maryland

I like art, music and gym because they're the most fun!
JESSICA BUTLER DANIELS, 11
Mystic, Connecticut

57

TOP Secret Journal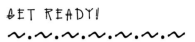

ON THE OUTSIDE IT LOOKS JUST LIKE A COOL, HANDMADE JOURNAL, BUT OPEN THE COVER AND VOILA! IT'S LIKE A MAZE DESIGNED TO CONFUSE SNOOPERS! FLIPPING THROUGH THE PAGES YOU'LL FIND HIDDEN POCKETS AND SECRET ENVELOPES SPRINKLED IN RANDOM PLACES, MAKING THIS JOURNAL A GREAT PLACE TO STASH YOUR PRIVATE NOTES, PHOTOS, OR DOODLES.

GET READY!
~.~.~.~.~.~.~

30 or more sheets of paper (the more variety the better), 8½ × 11 inches (21.6 × 27.9 cm)

Several extra sheets of decorative paper (for the secret pouches), 8½ × 11 inches (21.6 × 27.9 cm)

Decorative ribbon, measuring at least 24 inches (61 cm) long, not more than ¼ inch (6 mm) wide

Pencil

Ruler

Scissors

Hand-held hole punch

Paper clips (optional)

Craft glue

1. Separate the journal's pages into three equal piles. Cut the pages in one pile to 6 × 11 inches (15.2 × 27.9 cm), another to 7 ¼ × 11 inches (18.4 × 27.9 cm), and leave the third pile at 8 ½ × 11 inches (21.6 × 27.9 cm). Keep the piles separate.

2. Take a piece of paper from your first stack and measure ½ inch (1.3 cm) from the top and bottom of the left-hand side. Mark the spot with a dot. Measure 1 inch (2.5 cm) down from the dot and mark again. Continue down the length of the page until there are 11 marked dots. Place the remaining pages in your first stack behind the first marked page. Line the pages up, then punch through the dots with a hole punch. Continue this process with the remaining two piles of journal pages.

3. To make a hidden pouch, you'll need a sheet of the decorative 8 ½ × 11-inch (21.6 cm) paper. Fold the sheet in half, decorative side out. Put a thin line of glue along two of the edges, leaving one side unglued. Press the glued edges together firmly and allow to dry. Make more pouches this same way if you want. Place any finished pouches under one of the punched pages. Make sure the open side is not facing the left side. Punch through the top page, making holes in the pouch.

4. To make small envelopes, copy the template on the right, adjusting the size to fit your journal. Place the template on top of a sheet of decorative

paper. Trace around the edges of the template. Cut out the shape you drew, fold along the edges, and glue the sides together to form a small envelope. Brush glue along the back side of each envelope you make, and press down onto any page you choose.

5. Now align all of your punched pages, placing the largest pile at the bottom, the next in size on top of that, and the smallest pile of papers on the top (see Figure 1). Set the pouches throughout the book, lining up their holes with those of

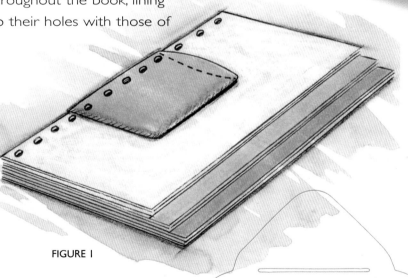

FIGURE 1

the pages. To keep the pages and their holes lined up, you may want to place a few paper clips along the edges of the journal. This will keep everything from shifting as you sew with the ribbon.

TEMPLATE

6. Starting at the back of the journal, pull the ribbon through the bottom hole, coming through the front cover page. Leave 1 to 2 inches (2.5 to 5.1 cm) of ribbon at the end. If you have a hard time getting the ribbon through the holes, poke it through using the point of your pencil.

7. Wrap the ribbon around the left edge of the journal, pull upward, and through the second hole in the back. The ribbon will be coming out of the front (see Figure 2). Continue stitching through the holes this way until the ribbon comes out the top hole.

8. Go around the edge of the journal and through the second-to-the-top hole in the back. The ribbon will be coming out the front of the journal. Continue stitching downward. When you reach the bottom, tie the remaining ribbon in a knot and trim off the ends.

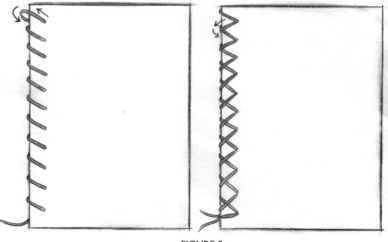

FIGURE 2

WANTED: CREATIVE, IMAGINATIVE PERSON!

IT'S NEVER TOO EARLY TO START THINKING ABOUT WHAT YOU WANT TO DO WHEN YOU GROW UP.

In fact, the things that you enjoy now are a good indication of what kind of work you'll choose to do in the future. If you can't wait to get home from school so you can start making a new bracelet or creating a mosaic on your floor, you may want to look into a career in the arts or design (or you could just keep making things as a hobby and become a surgeon). There's an old saying "If you love what you do, you'll never have to work a day in your life, because every day will be fun."

There are many, many different ways to apply your talent for design. Here are just a few career tracks to look into:

ARCHITECT

ART DIRECTOR

COSTUME DESIGNER

FASHION DESIGNER

FLORAL DESIGNER

GRAPHIC DESIGNER

INDUSTRIAL DESIGNER

INTERIOR DESIGNER

JEWELRY DESIGNER

SET DESIGNER

TEXTILE DESIGNER

Find a mentor who is doing a job you think you might like, and ask her for advice. She may even invite you to spend a day at work with her so you can find out what her job is really like.

Check out these websites for more information about career mentors, and women in the arts and design.

MENTORS

www.womenswork.org

Take a look at the women artists section.

ARTS AND DESIGN CAREERS

www.yourcreativefuture.com

This site tells about jobs in different creative careers and features interviews with professionals. There's also a resource list and links to other websites.

Flashy Backpack ❁ ❁

SEQUIN APPLIQUÉS LOOK GREAT, BUT THEY CAN BE EXPENSIVE. YOU COULD SPEND A BUNDLE COLLECTING ENOUGH TO BEAUTIFY YOUR BACKPACK. OR YOU COULD BE CREATIVE AND GO TO THE SOURCE OF ALL GOOD MATERIALS—YOUR MOM'S CLOSET!

Maybe Mom has an old formal dress that she'll never wear again. It could be a gold mine of rhinestones, sequins, and beautiful beads (make sure you ask her before you make that first cut with your scissors!). Or how about your own closet? Maybe you have some of your old dance recital costumes laying around. Why not get some use out of them?

If your house is completely sequin-free, head down to your local thrift store and see what you can find. Look through the old dress racks. You're bound to find some wonderful beads, rhinestones, and sequins on old dresses. For a few bucks you'll walk away with enough cool stuff to make your backpack glimmer and shine.

When cutting sequin appliqués from a garment, be very careful. You want to avoid cutting the thread that holds all the sequins together. Turn the garment over to see where the stitching is around the appliqués. When you cut the appliqués, leave as much of a fabric border around them as you can. You can go in and carefully trim the fabric away later.

To attach sequin appliqués to a backpack, just use tacky glue. Use your imagination and come up with a one-of-a-kind design. Let the glue set overnight.

62

ʼlad About Magnets

IN A PERFECT
WORLD, YOU'D BE
ABLE TO DO ANYTHING
YOU WANT TO THE
INSIDE OF YOUR LOCKER.
YOU COULD PAINT IT PURPLE,
LINE IT IN FAKE FUR, OR INSTALL
A SOUND SYSTEM.
UNFORTUNATELY, SCHOOLS HAVE
RULES ABOUT THOSE SORTS OF THINGS,
SO YOU'LL HAVE TO SETTLE FOR A
LESS PERMANENT LOCKER
MAKEOVER. MAGNETS ARE THE
PERFECT STYLE SOLUTION! YOU
CAN DECORATE THEM, REARRANGE
THEM ON A WHIM, USE THEM TO
HOLD NOTES, PICTURES,
OR MAGAZINE COL-
LAGES. THESE ARE JUST A
FEW IDEAS. YOU'RE SURE
TO COME UP WITH MORE. GO
MAGNET MAD!

GET READY!
~.~.~.~.~.~.~

Magnets with peel-and-stick backing in small sizes, on sheets or in rolls

Scissors

Hot glue gun and glue sticks

TAKE YOUR PICK
~.~.~.~.~.~.~

Silk flowers

Star sequins

Plastic jewels

Flat marbles

Magazine pictures or words

Holographic paper

Origami paper

Large metallic gift ribbons

14-gauge copper wire

Craft glue

Flower and Jewel Magnets

Attach your flowers or jewels to magnets with hot glue. To make the ones with the sequin stars, hot glue the jewel to the star first, then hot glue the star to the magnet. Easy, easy, easy!

63

Sparkly Metallic Gift Ribbon Magnets 🌀

Hot glue the gift ribbon to the magnet. For the photo and memo holder magnets, cut a 24-inch (61 cm) piece of copper wire, fold it in half, and coil the ends into spirals. Stick the wire through the middle of the gift ribbon, and attach both pieces to the magnet with hot glue. Just slide your pictures or notes through the spirals!

Flat Marble Magnets 🌀

Cut out pictures, words, or patterns from magazines, or cut small pieces of holographic or origami paper about the size of your flat marbles. Use craft glue that dries clear to glue the paper to the flat side of the marble. Let it dry for about 20 minutes, then trim the excess paper so there's none sticking out on the sides. Attach a magnet to the flat back side of the marble.

Tin Bins 🌀

WHAT DO YOU DO WITH THOSE EMPTY CANDY AND MINT TINS WHEN ALL THE SWEET STUFF INSIDE THEM IS GONE? MAGNETIZE THEM AND MAKE AN ORGANIZING SYSTEM FOR YOUR LOCKER! YOU'VE GOT TONS OF TINY THINGS TO KEEP TRACK OF DURING YOUR SCHOOL DAY—CHANGE, HAIR CLIPS, CANDY, NOTES FROM YOUR FRIENDS. STORE IT ALL IN CUTE DECORATED MINT TINS. YOU CAN EMBELLISH THEM WITH JUST ABOUT ANYTHING—SPRAY PAINT, GLITTER, NAIL POLISH, DIMENSIONAL PAINT, OR COLLAGE. THEN JUST STICK A MAGNET ON THE BACK, HANG IT IN YOUR LOCKER, AND WAIT TO HEAR YOUR FRIENDS SAY "COOOL! WHERE'D YOU GET THAT?"

P.S. THEY ALSO MAKE GREAT FRAMES!

GET READY!
~.~.~.~.~.~.~.~

Empty mint or candy tins

Sandpaper

Heavy-duty magnets

TAKE YOUR PICK
~.~.~.~.~.~.~.~

Spray paint

Nail polish (colored, glitter, and clear)

Dimensional paint

Glitter

Rhinestones or plastic jewels

Tacky glue

Paper bag

Magazine cutouts

Holographic paper

Photos of friends

1. Clean out the mint or candy residue from the inside of the tin.

2. Scuff up the surface of the tin with sandpaper. You don't have to take all the paint off, but having a rough surface helps the paint or nail polish stick better.

3. Decorate your tin! Spray paint works well. Work over a flat surface outside, so you don't get drips or inhale fumes. Try a solid-colored paint first, and then a glitter spray over it (you'll need to wait about 30 minutes between coats). When the paint dries, seal it with clear nail polish to prevent chipping.

Colored nail polish also looks great. Paint the whole tin with a solid color first, then when it dries, you can apply designs in other colors, or add a coat of glitter nail polish. When you're happy with your design, apply a coat of clear nail polish.

You could also try covering your tin in glitter. Just spray paint your tin, apply a thick coat of craft glue to the top of the tin, fill a paper bag with glitter, then put your tin inside it and shake it around. When you open the bag up, the top of the tin will be covered in glitter.

Collage is fun, too. Flip through magazines, cut out pictures, patterns, or images that you like, and try them out on the top of the tin before actually gluing them on. When you have the arrangement you like, apply glue to the backs of the cutouts and glue them to the tin.

4. Cut a big piece of magnet and attach it to the back of your tin. It will have to be fairly large to support the weight of your tin plus the items inside it when hanging in your locker.

5. Hang your tin in your locker, and start storing stuff! If you have a cute picture of your friends, glue it to the inside of your tin so that you'll see their faces each time you open it up!

Friendly Face Zipper Pulls

A ZIPPER PULL IS A FUN WAY TO ADD SOME INTEREST TO A HO-HUM BACKPACK. MAKE YOUR BACKPACK REALLY STAND OUT WITH A ONE-OF-A-KIND ZIPPER PULL FEATURING YOUR FRIEND'S FACE! EVEN IF YOU DON'T GET TO SEE YOUR FRIEND ALL DAY AT SCHOOL, YOU CAN SEE HER FACE RIGHT THERE ON YOUR ZIPPER PULL! THESE MAKE GREAT PRESENTS, TOO.

Get Ready!
~.~.~.~.~.~.~

Black and white photocopies (not laserjet copies) of your favorite photos

Polymer clay

Old rolling pin or brayer

Drinking glass or cookie cutters

Pencil

Scissors

Spoon

Ovenproof glass dish

Oven

Bamboo skewer

Clay cutter

Clip hook

1. Make black and white photocopies of your favorite photos. You can also scan any photos with your computer. Laser printer copies just won't work. If you print out something on a laser printer, take it to a copy store (or your parent's office) and make photocopies. Reduce or enlarge the photo to the size you need. The fresher the copies, the better the transfer.

2. Knead a block of polymer clay with your hands. Pull it apart, and squish it back together again. Knead it until it is soft and warm.

3. Flatten the clay with the palm of your hand. Then use the rolling pin (or brayer) to roll the clay. Make a couple of passes with the rolling pin, then lift the clay and turn it over. Repeat the process until your clay is the thickness you want.

4. Use cookie cutters or a drinking glass to cut a shape out of the clay.

5. Place the cookie cutter or glass on the photocopy. Trace around the shape with a pencil and cut it out.

6. Place the photocopy, image side down, on the clay. Gently rub the paper on the clay with the back of a spoon. Make sure all of the paper touches the clay. Keep rubbing, but don't squish the clay!

7. Let the transfer set for 15 minutes. Meanwhile, get an adult to turn on the oven to the temperature recommended by the clay manufacturer.

8. Pick up the clay and paper and put it in a glass baking dish. Poke a hole in the top of the clay with the bamboo skewer. Rub the paper once more.

9. Bake the clay according to the manufacturer's instructions.

10. Remove the dish from the oven. Peel off the paper, and let the clay cool completely.

11. Add other colors of clay in different shapes to the edges if you like. Roll out long, skinny coils or shape tiny balls. Flatten out the clay and use decorative cutters to cut out shapes. Add these shapes around the edges of the clay shapes you already baked. Press them firmly, but don't flatten them. Then, re-bake the clay.

12. Loop a hook through the hole in the top of the zipper pull, and hang it on your zipper!

P.S. You can also make magnets out of these!

DO IT YOURSELF! SAVE THE PLANET!

TEN WAYS TO MAKE IT YOURSELF AND HELP THE PLANET

Did you know that 20% of the world's population consumes 80% of the world's resources? Or that you personally create about 1,000 pounds of garbage a year?* Pretty scary, huh? There are lots of ways that you can help to create less waste in this world and use resources more wisely. Making things yourself is fun, and it helps the planet! Here are some ways that you can make a difference:

1. Use old clothes to make new things. You can take some old jeans that are too small and make them into a shoulder bag (see page 103), or take an old skirt and jazz it up with a boa (see page 100). Before you throw something out, think about why you liked it in the first place. If you like the fabric, you can always take it apart and use it for something else. Using something old means that a new thing isn't being made, and that saves energy and resources.

2. There's a lot of packaging in this world, and a lot of it gets thrown away. Before you toss it, think about another use for your package. Old shoe boxes are great for storage if you decorate them with collage or fabric trim. You can decorate plain old film containers and use them as perfume and glitter containers (see pages 74-76). Empty mint or candy tins can be used for organizing little things (see page 64-65).

3. You can make presents for friends instead of buying them (see pages 40 to 87). Presents you make are always more special, and your friends will appreciate the effort you took to make something unique for them. It's a gift from the heart!

4. When you get presents from others, save the wrapping paper and use it in collage, or reuse it to wrap another present. You can decoupage it to a bottle to make a cool vase, or spray glue it to your bulletin board to put a cool background over the ordinary cork one. Cut out the images from the greeting cards you get and use them in collage too! Cut up magazines to decorate stuff with, too.

5. You can take an ordinary household object and turn it into something cool (see safety pin bracelets on page 108-109). Make bracelets from rubber bands. A lot of useful things are just lying around your house anyway. Put them to good use!

6. Instead of buying all new craft materials, you can use things that you find in nature, like smooth river pebbles, wildflowers, etc. Stuff in your own backyard is free! Stuff in other people's backyards or on public property is off limits, though!

7. Make some new accessories to go with your old clothes instead of buying all new outfits. Your handmade accessories will be totally unique. A scarf, a hat, or a bracelet is all you need to transform an old outfit. You can easily make hair accessories (see pages 97-99) that will give you a new look for less money.

8. Shop at thrift stores and flea markets—you'll save money and keep another new thing from coming into this world. Plus, it's fun! You can learn a lot about history from seeing how thing were made in the past and what was in fashion at various periods of time.

9. Instead of asking your parents for new furniture, get out some paint and glitter. Make new handles for your dresser drawers (see page 27). Or do a collage on the top of a table. Use chalkboard or magnetic paint on a headboard or desktop. Add fringe to the edge of your bookshelf. You won't even recognize your old furniture when you're done with it!

10. Don't believe the hype! You don't have to wear expensive clothes or have a brand new everything to be cool. Use what you've got, and be self-sufficient, creative, and one-of-a-kind!

✿ Figures from the New Roadmap Foundation

67

A) STAND IN LINE AT THE BATH-ROOM MIRROR BEHIND THE OLDER GIRLS, GO TO CLASS LATE, AND GET IN TROUBLE;

B) PUT ON A HAT AND HOPE HE'S SICK TODAY; OR

C) MAKE A QUICK STOP AT YOUR LOCKER, CHECK YOUR LOOK IN YOUR LOCKER MIRROR, FRESHEN UP, AND GET TO CLASS ON TIME, LOOKIN' GORGEOUS.

YES, GIRLS, THE ANSWER IS C. WITH A COOL LOCKER MIRROR, CHECKING YOUR LOOK AT SCHOOL IS NOT A PROBLEM. MAKE A CUTE MIRROR, AND CARRY ON WITH CONFIDENCE!

GET READY!
~.~.~.~.~.~.~

Flower-shaped craft-foam framed mirror

Dimensional paint

 craft stores or discount stores

1. Make small dots of paint around the outside border of the mirror, alternating the colors.

2. Outline the outer edge of each petal with small dots of paint, using a separate color for each petal. You're done! And you look fabulous, dahling!

Locker Luau

IN YOUR CRAZY SCHOOL DAY, YOU'VE GOT ONE OASIS— ONE LITTLE PLACE IN THE WHOLE SCHOOL TO CALL YOUR OWN—AT LEAST UNTIL THEY CHANGE THE COMBINA-TION AT THE END OF THE YEAR. IT'S YOUR LOCKER! YOUR HOME AWAY FROM HOME. MAKE IT A HAPPY PLACE! THIS ORGANIZER STORES YOUR STUFF, KEEPS YOUR LIFE TOGETHER, AND MAKES YOU SMILE BEFORE YOU RUN OFF TO YOUR NEXT CLASS.

GET READY!
~.~.~.~.~.~.~

Plastic-coated wire mesh organizer basket

Large pack of raffia

Scissors

Craft foam sheet

Hot glue gun and glue sticks

Tropical silk flowers and leaves

Hawaiian lady cutout (optional)

Heavy-duty magnets

Check Your Look Locker Mirror

LET'S TAKE A LITTLE QUIZ: YOUR CRUSH IS IN YOUR NEXT PERIOD CLASS. YOU HAVE JUST FINISHED GYM CLASS, AND THE HAIRDO YOU HAD THIS MORNING IS NOW A HAIR-DON'T. YOU:

1. Gather four pieces of raffia and fold them in half once, and then again. Wrap the raffia around the top of the basket, then thread the raffia back through itself and pull tight (see illustration, above). Repeat until the entire basket is covered in raffia (it should look like a grass skirt!).

2. Weave more raffia around the top of the basket to hide any part of the basket you can still see. Trim the edges of the skirt so that it ends at the bottom of the basket.

3. Line the inside of the basket with the craft foam sheet. Cut off any foam that hangs over the edges. Hot glue the craft foam inside the top of the basket.

4. Hot glue the tropical silk flowers, leaves, and the Hawaiian lady to the raffia on the front of your basket.

5. Attach the magnets to the plastic-coated wire on the back of the basket. Stick the basket to your locker, and say Aloha to fun!

69

YOUR FRIENDS ARE A BIG PART OF YOUR WORLD! THEY ARE THERE TO SHARE FUN TIMES WITH YOU. THEY LISTEN TO YOU WHEN YOU HAVE A PROBLEM. THEY KEEP YOUR SECRETS. TOGETHER, YOU AND YOUR FRIENDS FACE LIFE'S UPS AND DOWNS.

Friends

Making presents for your friends is a great way to show them how much they mean to you. It shows that you care enough to give them your time, your effort, and your imagination.

The only thing more fun than making things for your friends is making things *with* them! Spending time together and making cool stuff will bring you and your friends closer and create great memories for you to share.

In this section of the book, you'll learn how to make awesome presents that your friends will love. You'll also find ideas for making stuff at parties or sleepovers. From homemade beauty products to magical, mystical dream pillows, you'll find something that you and your friends will enjoy making together. There are even some things to make for your pet friends, too!

Friends Forever Jewelry!!

GET READY!

- 1 polymer clay cane for each guest ☞
- Solid-color polymer clay
- Craft knife with sharp blades (to cut clay canes)
- Ruler
- Wooden skewers or stiff wire
- Baking pan
- Oven
- Polymer clay glaze
- Small artist paintbrush
- Elastic cord, plastic cord, hemp, or other material for stringing beads
- Beads
- Earring fronts and backs 🕷
- Super-strong epoxy

☞ *You only need about half a cane to make 6 to 10 beads, so slice each cane in half and use the rest later for other projects.*

🕷 *craft stores*

YOU KNOW YOU'VE HAD A GREAT PARTY WHEN EVERYONE GOES HOME HAPPY. THINK HOW GREAT YOUR PARTY WOULD BE IF EVERYONE WENT HOME HAPPY AND WITH NEW JEWELRY TO WEAR, TOO! HERE'S HOW TO MAKE IT HAPPEN: GET A POLYMER CLAY CANE IN A DIFFERENT PATTERN FOR EACH FRIEND AT YOUR PARTY. EACH GIRL CAN MAKE EARRINGS IN A PATTERN SHE CHOOSES, THEN MAKE BEADS IN THE SAME PATTERN TO SHARE WITH OTHER GUESTS. IN THE END, EVERYONE WILL HAVE NEW EARRINGS AND A BRACELET MADE FROM BEADS IN EACH GIRL'S PATTERN. IT'S A GREAT WAY TO REMEMBER YOUR FRIENDS AND THE GREAT TIME YOU HAD AT YOUR PARTY!

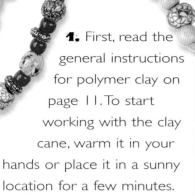

1. First, read the general instructions for polymer clay on page 11. To start working with the clay cane, warm it in your hands or place it in a sunny location for a few minutes.

2. Slowly roll the cane back and forth on a smooth surface to make it smaller. Turn it as you roll it so the shape doesn't become distorted. The ends of the cane may start to look squished, but don't worry. Take your time and roll carefully, and the design inside the cane will remain intact.

3. When the cane is about ⅜ inch (9.5 mm) in diameter, use a craft knife with a sharp blade to cut it into thin slices, each about ⅟₁₆-inch (1.6 mm) thick. Let the cane roll as you slice so the design doesn't get distorted.

4. Take a small piece of solid-color polymer clay and roll it into a ball that's slightly smaller than you'd like your bead to be.

5. Press one thin cane slice between your thumb and forefinger to warm it and to flatten its edges slightly, then press the slice onto the ball of solid-color clay. Arrange more slices onto the ball until the entire surface is covered.

6. Roll the ball gently between your hands to create a round bead with a smooth surface.

7. Pierce the center of each bead with a skewer or length of stiff wire. As you make more beads, add them to the skewer or wire, but leave a little space between each one. When all your beads are made, suspend the skewers or wires across the top of a baking pan.

8. To make the earrings, take two slices from the cane and place them in the bottom of the pan. Bake the beads and the earring slices following the manufacturer's directions.

9. After the beads and earring slices have cooled, apply a thin coat of the polymer clay glaze to one side of each earring, and all over each bead (it will be easy to glaze the beads if you keep them on the skewer or wire).

10. Once the beads have dried (usually in about an hour), have each friend give the other guests one bead made from her cane. String these, along with other beads, onto the elastic, plastic, or hemp cord to make a bracelet.

11. To make earrings, simply glue the unglazed sides of your cane slices onto earring backs and let them dry.

Spa Party!

YOU KNOW THAT BEAUTY COMES FROM WITHIN, BUT DID YOU KNOW THAT BEAUTY PRODUCTS DON'T HAVE TO COME FROM A STORE? YOU CAN MAKE THEM AT HOME IN YOUR OWN KITCHEN, SAVE YOURSELF A BUNCH OF MONEY, AND HAVE A BLAST.

PAMPER YOURSELF AND YOUR FRIENDS WITH A SPA PARTY WHERE YOU MAKE YOUR OWN BEAUTY PRODUCTS. YOU CAN PICK YOUR OWN FLAVORS, SCENTS, AND COLORS, EXPERIMENT UNTIL YOU'VE GOT THE RECIPE JUST RIGHT, THEN CREATE A TOTALLY UNIQUE CONTAINER FOR STORING YOUR NEW CONCOCTION. CHECK OUT THESE RECIPES!

A single rose can be my garden, a single friend, my world.

LEO BUSCAGLIA

73

Glossy Posse Lip Gloss

DON'T YOU LOVE LIP GLOSS? IT'S FUN, IT'S SHIMMERY, AND IT LOOKS AND SMELLS GREAT! DID YOU KNOW YOU CAN MAKE YOUR OWN IN JUST A FEW MINUTES? FIRST, MAKE A COOL CONTAINER FOR YOUR GLOSS, THEN LET THE REAL FUN BEGIN—MIXING, MELTING, AND MAKING YOUR OWN BRAND OF LIP GLOSS! THIS IS TWO GREAT PROJECTS IN ONE!

GET READY!
~.~.~.~.~.~.~

Small, round, metal containers or pillboxes

Plastic jewels

Silver spray paint

Hot glue gun and glue sticks

Glitter

Dimensional paint

Mixing bowl or container

Beeswax

Cocoa butter

Sweet almond oil

Coconut oil

TAKE YOUR PICK
~.~.~.~.~.~.~

Peppermint oil

Almond oil

Flavor extracts, such as vanilla or lemon (from the grocery store)

Breath freshener drops (from a drug store)

Old lipstick and eye shadow

 health food stores

1. Let's start with the containers so they'll be ready to use when you've finished making the gloss. If you can't find pill containers, try to find the little metal containers that bindi come in (those little Indian jewel dots that you can put on your face or body). Spray paint the container of your choice, and hot glue the jewels to the top. Trace around the jewels with dimensional paint if you want. Allow everything to dry (this should take a few hours).

2. Now you're ready to make the gloss. In a small container mix:

1 ½ teaspoons (7.5 mL) beeswax

1 teaspoon (5 mL) cocoa butter

1 teaspoon (5 mL) sweet almond oil

1 teaspoon (5 mL) coconut oil

3. Heat the mixture in the microwave for 45 seconds. If it doesn't melt completely, heat it again in 20-second intervals. The goal is to melt the beeswax without heating it too high. Add 8 to 10 drops of the flavoring of your choice. If you want

74

color in your gloss, melt in a little bit of old lipstick, or drop in a dab of old powder eye shadow or ultrafine glitter. Don't overdo it!

4. Pour the gloss into the containers (this recipe will fill one or two, depending on the size), and allow it to cool. If you want to make more, double or triple the recipe, and add different flavors.

The only way to have a friend is to be one.

RALPH WALDO EMERSON, 1841

Perfumania!

YOU AND YOUR FRIENDS CAN MAKE YOUR OWN UNIQUE FRAGRANCE IN A SOLID PERFUME. EACH GIRL CAN EXPERIMENT WITH ESSENTIAL OILS TO PICK THE FRAGRANCE THAT IS POSITIVELY HER! YOU CAN EACH GIVE YOUR PERFUME A NAME LIKE "LINDSEY'S LOVELY LAVENDER" OR "ALLISON'S AMAZING ORANGE BLOSSOM." THE FUN PART IS DECORATING THE PERFUME CONTAINERS. THEY'RE JUST OLD FILM CANISTERS DRESSED UP TO EXPRESS THE GIRL WHO MADE THEM!

GET READY!

Stovetop

Double boiler

1 tablespoon (15 mL) beeswax

3 tablespoons (45 mL) sweet almond oil 🐾

30 to 40 drops of essential oil, such as lavender, orange, patchouli, rose, gardenia 🐾

Empty film canisters ☜

🐾 *health food stores*

☜ *Some people are afraid there are chemicals in these. That's not true, but wash them out before you use them just so everyone can be comfortable.*

TAKE YOUR PICK

Craft foam

Ribbon trim

Glitter

Plastic jewels

Buttons

Feathers

Nail polish (glitter, colored, and clear)

Holographic paper with peel-and-stick backing

Tacky glue

Craft glue

Finials

Wooden drawer knobs

75

1. Set up a double boiler on your stove. That means you'll have one pot with water in it (on the bottom), and you'll place another pot on top of it for your ingredients. The double boiler prevents the ingredients from having direct contact with heat.

2. Pour water into your first pot, and turn on your stove to medium heat. Put your second pot inside the first one, and pour in your sweet almond oil, then add your beeswax (it usually comes in small solid pieces).

3. Let the beeswax melt, then add your essential oil. You can use one scent or make a mix of several of your favorites. Stir well to make sure everything is mixed, then turn off the heat.

4. Pour your mixture into an empty film canister until you reach the top. Wait a few minutes. If your cannister is clear, you'll see the wax starting to turn solid

from the bottom of the canister up. You'll also notice that as the mixture becomes solid, the level goes down a little. If you have a little left in your pot, pour it in to level it off (you'll have to do this fairly soon or the leftover will also turn solid).

5. Now decorate your film canisters! You can cut holographic paper and wrap it around the canister, glue ribbon or craft foam around it, glue plastic jewels on it, coat it in glue and roll it in glitter, or paint it with nail polish. The possibilities are endless! You can glue a button onto the lid, or hot glue a round drawer pull (painted with glitter nail polish). You could also draw a face on a drawer pull knob and add button lips! You can use finials (those little things you put on the end of curtain rods) to make an elegant lid, or hot glue a porcelain doll's head to the top. Have a bunch of materials on hand and let every friend decorate her own!

6. To use your perfume, just rub some on your finger, then dab it on your wrists or neck!

Glamour Girl Glitter

OK, NOW YOUR LIPS ARE SHINY AND YOU SMELL GREAT. WHAT'S NEXT? GLITTER GEL! YOU CAN PUT IT ON YOUR FACE, YOUR SHOULDERS, IN YOUR HAIR, OR EVEN ON YOUR FEET!

GET READY!
~.~.~.~.~.~.~.~

4 teaspoons (20 mL) aloe vera gel (the stuff you use to soothe a sunburn) 🐞

A dab of petroleum jelly (optional)

Small bowl

Spoon

Ultrafine glitter

Empty film canister

TAKE YOUR PICK
~.~.~.~.~.~.~.~

Any of the things you used to decorate your perfume containers

🐞 *drug stores or discount stores*

1. Spoon the aloe vera gel into a bowl. Add a tiny dab of petroleum jelly to make your mixture a little thicker.

2. Put a few pinches of glitter into your mixture. Mix it around, then test it on the back of your hand or your wrist to see how much glitter shows up. Keep mixing in more glitter until you're satisfied with the results. You don't need much to make an impact!

3. Pour the mixture into a film canister. You may need to add a little more aloe vera gel to get the mixture to the top of the canister. Mix it all around again.

4. Decorate your film canister as described in the perfume instructions. Put on your glitter, and glow, glow, glow!

The Clean Scene: Cool Soap!!

YOUR AMAZING COLLECTION OF HOMEMADE BEAUTY PRODUCTS WOULD NOT BE COMPLETE WITHOUT THE FINISHING TOUCH: A FABULOUSLY FRAGRANT, SENSATIONAL, IRRESISTIBLE BAR OF HOMEMADE SOAP.

GET READY!
~.~.~.~.~.~.~

Glycerine cakes in different colors ☛

Kitchen knife with wide smooth blade

Wooden spoon

Microwaveproof container

Fragrance oil for soapmaking ✿

Color additive for soapmaking ✿

Ground oatmeal (optional)

Mold, such as a cookie cutter, soapmaking or candle mold

Rectangular bread pan

(microwaveproof glass or plastic)

Microwave oven

Butter knife

☛ You'll need about 2½ glycerine cakes to make one loaf of soap. You can get about seven slices of soap out of each loaf.

✿ You can get these supplies from sources on the Internet. Make sure to use products made especially for soapmaking. Don't use food coloring or essential oils for your soap—they don't work well and can bother people with sensitive skin.

77

1. Make the inserts for the soaps first (you can do this a day in advance to save time). Cut up your glycerine cakes into cubes. Put the cubes in a microwaveproof container, then melt them in a microwave for 2 to 3 minutes. Stir the mixture, then put it in the microwave again for another 2 to 3 minutes. Stir the mixture, and return it to the microwave again. You'll need to keep stirring and melting for about 8 minutes total. Keep stirring until the mixture is smooth.

2. Add your color and fragrance to the mixture gradually, drop by drop, but as quickly as you can. The mixture will be cooling and you need get the color and fragrance in before a film sets over the top (usually in about 5 minutes). You'll need about 2½ table-spoons (37 mL) of color and fragrance total for a big loaf of soap.

3. Pour the mixture into your pan. If you want specific shapes, like hearts, put cookie cutters or other molds inside the pan first. If you have candle or soap-

making molds, just pour the mixture directly into the molds. Put the mixture in the refrigerator and let it set for at least 6 hours. Cut around the molds to remove the inserts from the rest of the loaf. If you didn't use inserts, just cut the loaf into small shapes.

4. Make your "main" soap loaf following the same directions for the inserts. Let it cool for just a few minutes. Don't pour the mixture into the pan yet.

5. Put your inserts in the bottom of your pan and arrange them the way you want them—remember, you're making several slices, so you want to spread out your inserts so there are some in each slice. If you want to add oatmeal to your soap, pour a layer onto the bottom of the pan. Pour your mixture into the pan. If bubbles form on the top of the mixture after you've poured, scoop them out with a spoon. Put your pan in the refrigerator and let it set for 4 or 5 hours.

7. Run a butter knife around the edge of your pan to separate the soap

loaf from the pan. Flip the container over and bang on the bottom to knock the loaf out, the same way you would take a cake from a pan.

8. Use the kitchen knife to slice the loaf into bars of soap and share them with your friends!

Friendship is a golden chain, the links are friends so dear, and like a rare and precious jewel, it's treasured more each year.

Dream Pillows

CULTURES AROUND THE WORLD BELIEVE THAT HERBS CAN HEAL ILLNESSES AND EVEN INFLUENCE YOUR DREAMS. CERTAIN HERBS ARE SAID TO INSPIRE CERTAIN KINDS OF DREAMS (SEE STORY ON PAGE 81). DREAM PILLOWS ARE A FUN WAY TO LEARN ABOUT HERBS AND DREAMS, AND THEY MAKE GREAT GIFTS FOR YOUR FRIENDS. TRY MAKING DREAM PILLOWS WITH YOUR FRIENDS AT A SLEEPOVER. YOU CAN EACH MAKE A PILLOW AND COMPARE YOUR DREAMS IN THE MORNING! YOUR PILLOW WILL REMAIN FRAGRANT FOR ABOUT SIX MONTHS AND CAN BE REFRESHED WITH ESSENTIAL OILS.

Friendship consists of forgetting what one gives and remembering what one receives.

DUMAS THE YOUNGER

⌐ET READY!
~.~.~.~.~.~.~.~

**FOR EACH PILLOW
YOU NEED:**
....

¼ yard (22.9 cm) fabric of your choice (celestial prints are good)

¼ yard (22.9 cm) lining fabric

Scissors

Straight pins

Sewing needle and thread

Sewing machine (optional)

3 cups (600 g) of flaxseed 🌟

½ cup (100 g) chamomile 🌟

½ cup (100 g) lavender 🌟

¼ cup (50 g) hops 🌟

¼ cup (50 g) mugwort 🌟

¼ cup (50 g) spearmint 🌟

Bowl and funnel

🌟 *health food stores*

Note: These instructions are for hand-sewing, but you can easily sew the pillow on a sewing machine if you have one.

1. Cut the fabric and lining fabric to the size of your choice (the one in the picture is a 12-inch [30.5 cm] square). Cut the fabric ½ inch (1.3 cm) wider and longer than you want your pillow, so you'll have enough fabric for the hem.

2. Lay your printed fabric face down with the lining fabric on top of it.

3. Fold the fabric in half with the lining side on the outside.

4. Pin the fabric and lining to keep them together, about 1 inch (2.5 cm) in from the edge.

5. Hand sew around three sides of the pillow, about ½ inch (1.3 cm) in from the edge. Don't sew the folded edge. Leave about 2 inches (5.1 cm) open on your last side so you can stuff the pillow.

6. Pull your pillow inside out through the opening hole. Now your printed fabric is on the outside.

7. Mix all your herbs and flaxseed in a bowl.

8. Put the narrow end of the funnel in the pillow opening and pour the herbs inside.

9. Tuck the fabric in and sew the opening closed.

Eye Pillows

EYE PILLOWS ARE GREAT AT THE END OF THE DAY, WHEN YOU'VE BEEN DOING HOMEWORK FOR HOURS AND STARING AT YOUR COMPUTER SCREEN, OR JUST WHEN YOU NEED TO RELAX. YOU CAN MAKE AN EYE PILLOW THE SAME WAY YOU MADE THE DREAM PILLOW—JUST MAKE IT ABOUT HALF THE SIZE.

To make a soothing eye pillow, follow the instructions for the dream pillow, but use this herbal recipe inside the pillow instead:

1 ½ cups (300 g) flaxseed

¼ cup (50 g) camomile

¼ cup (50 g) eucalyptus

¼ cup (50 g) spearmint

Pinch of hops

All of these ingredients can be found at health food stores.

N YOUR DREAMS

CIENTISTS HAVE BEEN STUDYING FOR YEARS TO FIND OUT WHAT HAPPENS WHEN WE SLEEP, AND THEY STILL DON'T KNOW ALL THE ANSWERS.

There are many different theories on why we have dreams and what our dreams mean, but much remains unknown. In many cultures, people believe that herbs can influence your dreams. In some parts of Mexico, there's even an herb called *Calea Zacatechichi*, "the dream herb," which people put in tea. After drinking the tea, you are supposed to fall asleep, and your dream will help you answer a question or find things that you've lost. Do you think an herb can influence your dreams? Make a dream pillow (pages 79-80) and find out.

Here's a list of herbs and the dreams they are supposed to inspire:

BASIL	Dreams of love and flying
LAVENDER	Peaceful dreams
LEMON	Happy dreams
JASMINE	Romantic dreams
MUGWORT	Helps you remember your dreams
PEPPERMINT	Helps you see the future in your dreams
SAGE	Helps you find answers to your questions in your dreams
SPEARMINT	Vivid dreams
TUBEROSE	Romantic dreams

Keep a dream journal next to your bed, and write down your dreams in the morning first thing when you wake up. Look for more information on dream interpretation at the library or on the Internet so you can get some clues as to what your dreams mean.

riendship improves happiness, oubles our joys, and ivides our sorrow. JOSEPH ADDISON

What Do You Like to Do with Your Friends?

We like to hang out together and talk. We give each other friendship bracelets, have slumber parties, and do stuff like play Truth or Dare.

BRENDA LEE REYES, 11
Connecticut

My best friends are Nora, Kara, and Gloria. We talk together and play basketball, but mostly we just like to hang out with each other.

BRITTANY KO, 10
South Pasadena, CA

My closest friends are Maddy, Conley, Sue and Emily. Mostly what I like to do with them is make stuff, but with Maddy we sometimes write plays and act them out.

RACHEL WARRINER, 10
East Dummerston,
Vermont

Best Friends Forever Photo Album ◉

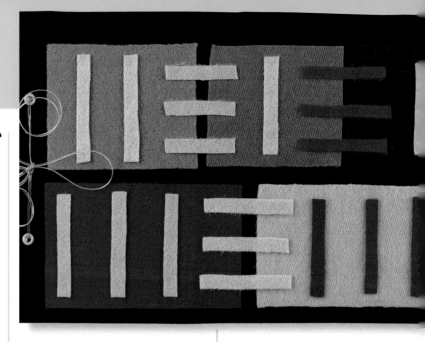

A PHOTO ALBUM IS A PERFECT GIFT TO GIVE A FRIEND TO REMIND HER OF ALL THE GOOD TIMES YOU'VE HAD TOGETHER. YOUR GIFT WILL BE EVEN MORE SPECIAL IF YOU MAKE THE ALBUM YOURSELF. YOU'LL BE SURPRISED HOW EASY IT IS TO MAKE. YOU CAN GET ALL YOUR MATERIALS AT A CRAFT STORE, COME UP WITH A ONE-OF-A-KIND DESIGN FEATURING YOUR FRIEND'S FAVORITE COLORS, AND FILL THE ALBUM PAGES WITH ALL YOUR FAVORITE PHOTOS.

GET READY!
~.~.~.~.~.~.~

2 pieces of stiffened felt

Ruler

Pencil

Scissors

Copy paper or construction paper for the pages

Hole punch

Eyelet punch and eyelets (optional)

Soft felt in different colors

Craft glue

Ribbon, shoelaces, yarn, or plastic lacing material

Photo mounts

1. Measure and mark two equal pieces of felt for your covers. We cut a sheet of stiffened felt in half, which made our cover about 8 × 12 inches (20.3 × 30.5 cm). You can make your album whatever size you wish. After you cut the cover, it's a good time to measure and cut your pages to fit.

2. Mark where you want to place two holes on the short side of one cover. Punch the holes with a hole punch. Mark and punch matching holes on the other cover. If you have an eyelet punch, you can set colorful eyelets to protect the holes from wear.

3. Decide how you want to decorate your cover. We cut small rectangles of felt and glued them to the

cover. After we glued the shapes on the cover, we placed a couple of heavy books on top and let the glue dry overnight. You could also cut out chunky letter shapes from felt and give your album a title, like "Best Friends Forever."

4. Use your cover as a template to mark and punch holes in your pages.

5. Stack your pages between the covers and thread a length of ribbon or lacing thread through the holes. Tie it off with a simple bow—just like you use to tie your shoes.

6. Use photo mounts to attach photos to the pages. If you are giving your friend a blank album, give her a box of photo mounts, too! She'll appreciate the album even more if she can put photos right into it.

Best Buds Box

THERE'S NOTHING LIKE A TRUE FRIEND—SOMEONE WHO SHARES YOUR UPS AND DOWNS, THE EXCITING TIMES AND THE EMBARRASSING MOMENTS, AND STICKS WITH YOU THROUGH IT ALL. YOUR BEST BUDS MEAN A LOT TO YOU. SHOW THEM HOW YOU FEEL WITH A SPECIAL BOX FULL OF LITTLE SYMBOLS OF YOUR FRIENDSHIP!

GET READY!
~.~.~.~.~.~.~

Metal box or any other kind of box with a lid

TAKE YOUR PICK
~.~.~.~.~.~.~

Photos of you and your friend

Stickers

Craft foam sheets

Fabric paint

Magnet sheet with peel-and-stick backing 🐾

Tacky glue

Decoupage medium

🐾 craft stores

FOR INSIDE THE BOX:
....

Small toy bear

Small bird (available at craft stores)

Rubber band

Marble

Eraser

Piece of gum

Fudge candy roll

Piece of rope

Mint

Piece of wire

Star sticker

Chocolate kiss

83

1. Decorate the outside of the box with photos or color photocopies of photos of you and your friend. Paint "Best Buds Box" or "Best Friends Forever" on the lid of the box. If you are using a metal box, you can apply adhesive magnetic sheets to the backs of photos and then place them onto the box.

2. Use stickers and other materials to decorate the outside of the box. To make a frame from a craft foam sheet, simply cut the material into a shape that's slightly larger than your photo or photocopy. Then cut out an inside window that's slightly smaller than your picture or photocopy.

Cut a piece of magnet and attach it to the back of the photo and the frame. Attach other decorations to the box with magnets or decoupage medium.

3. Fill the box with special reminders of your friendship and a note explaining what they mean. Here's an example:

A BEAR.....because you are my beary best friend

A BIRD.....to remind you to try your wings

A RUBBER BAND.....to remind you to stay flexible

A MARBLE.....in case you start to lose yours

AN ERASER..... because we all make mistakes

A PIECE OF GUM.....to remind you to stick with it

A FUDGE CANDY ROLL.....to remind you to roll with the punches

A PIECE OF ROPE ......in case you get to the end of yours

A MINT.....because you mean a mint to me

A PIECE OF WIRE.....because we all get bent out of shape sometimes

A STAR.....to remind you to shine

A CHOCOLATE KISS.....to remind you how sweet you are

4. Give the box to your friend!

on't Forget Your
Furry Friends

WHEN YOU MAKE A LIST OF ALL YOUR FRIENDS, DON'T FORGET YOUR FURRY ONES. CATS AND DOGS DESERVE PRESENTS TOO! THEY ARE ALWAYS THERE TO GREET YOU AT THE END OF A LONG DAY, CURL UP WITH YOU, LISTEN TO YOUR PROBLEMS, KEEP YOUR SECRETS, AND COMFORT YOU. SHOW THEM HOW MUCH YOU APPRECIATE THEM WITH SPE-CIAL GIFTS THAT YOU CAN MAKE YOURSELF.

Dynamic Dog Duo! Leash and Collar ◎

YOUR DOG WILL BE THE ENVY OF ALL DOGS IN THE NEIGH-BORHOOD WITH THIS OH-SO-CHIC MATCHING COLLAR AND LEASH SET. YOU CAN CHANGE RIBBONS ACCORD-ING TO YOUR MOOD: AN ANI-MAL PRINT, A RAINBOW RIB-BON, A HIPPIE LOOK.

GET READY!
~.~.~.~.~.~.~.~

Nylon dog leash

Nylon dog collar

Decorative ribbons (same width as leash and collar)

Measuring tape or ruler

Hook-and-loop fastener tape with peel-and-stick backing

Scissors

Fray retardant ☛

Nail or other sharp object (see collar instructions)

☛ keeps fabric from unraveling

FOR THE LEASH

1. Measure the leash from the point where the handle starts to the end where the clasp is attached. Cut a piece of ribbon 3 inches (7.6 cm) longer than your measurement, and spray fray retardant to the ends to keep them from unravel-ing. Allow to dry.

2. Hook-and-loop tape comes in strips, one for the hook side and one for the loop side. Cut small pieces

85

of the tape to match the width of your leash. Depending on the length of your leash, you need from eight to 12 pieces of both hooks and loops.

3. Put one of the loop pieces (fuzzy) about 1 inch (2.5 cm) in from the point where the leash handle begins, and another about 1 inch (2.5 cm) in from the end where the clasp is

attached. Add loop pieces every 3 to 4 inches (7.6 to 10.2 cm) in between on the smooth side of the leash.

4. Turn the leash over and put one loop piece about 2 to 3 inches (5.1 to 7.6 cm) in from the end of the leash where the clasp is attached, then turn the leash back over.

5. Set the ribbon, wrong side up, beside the leash and attach one hook piece of tape to the wrong side of the ribbon to match

each loop piece on the leash, including the one on the other side, near the clasp end of the leash.

6. Wait a few hours to make sure the hook-and-loop tape is firmly adhered to the leash and ribbons, then attach the ribbon to the leash by connecting the hook and loop pieces together.

FOR THE COLLAR

1. Use the same method you used to make the collar (use the loop tape on the collar for your dog's comfort), but this time the ribbon should start at the end of the collar where the holes are, and fold around the back a little to the place where the buckle starts.

2. You'll need to use a nail or another sharp object to poke holes in the ribbon in the spots where the collar has holes. If the holes close up (this happens with some ribbon), you can cut a slightly larger hole with scissors and apply fray retardant around its edges.

Glamour Puss Cat Bed

DO YOU EVER GET THE FEELING THAT YOUR CAT IS NO ORDINARY CAT? SHE'S SO ELEGANT, SO ALOOF— IN THE CAT WORLD, SHE COULD QUITE POSSIBLY BE A CELEBRITY DOESN'T SHE DESERVE A BED WORTHY OF HER STATUS? THIS CAT BED IS THE PERFECT SOLUTION. IT'S GLAMOROUS, YET COZY—THE PERFECT PLACE FO YOUR CAT TO CURL UP AND DO WHAT SHE DOES BEST—SLEEP! THERE ARE TWO WAYS TO MAKE THIS BED, SO PICK THE ONE THAT MATCHES YOUR SKILLS, AND LISTEN TO THE GRATEFUL PURRS OF YOUR CAT AS SHE BASKS IN HER NEW BED.

GET READY!
~·~·~·~·~·~·~·~

Fake fur, about 2 yards (1.8 m

Scissors

Sturdy needle and thread

Thimble

Old towel

Straight pins

Marker

1 round foam circle, 14 inches (48.3 cm) in diameter

Fabric glue (optional)

 fabric and craft stores

NOTE: If you really don't want to sew the cat bed, just substitute fabric glue for a needle and thread. You'll need to let the glue set for at least a day in order for it to bond correctly.

1. Take the 12 × 60-inch (30.5 cm × 1.52 m) piece of fabric and fold it, right sides together, into a 6 × 60-inch (15.2 cm × 1.52 m) rectangle. Pin the 60-inch (1.52 m) ends of the fabric together. Use the needle and thread to sew a straight seam along that edge. Remove the pins when you're done.

2. Turn the fabric inside out. You'll have a long tube that's open at both ends.

3. Fold your towel until it's about 5 × 60 inches (12.7 cm × 1.52 m). Insert it into the fabric tube, then reach through the tube and pull the towel to the other end.

4. Pins the ends of the tube together, then sew a strong seam where the two ends meet.

5. Fold the 20 × 40-inch (50.8 cm × 1 m) piece of fake fur in half to form a 20-inch (50.8 cm) square. Draw a circle on the top side of the square. Hold the top and bottom squares together as you cut through both layers along your marked line to make two circles.

6. Place one circle on top of the other, right sides together. Pin the two pieces together.

7. Sew a seam around the outside of the circle, but leave about 7 inches (17.8 cm) of the circle unsewn.

8. Remove the pins and turn the fabric right side out. Insert the round piece of foam into the opening.

9. Fold in the unsewn edges of the fabric at the opening, and pin them together. Sew along the edges to close up the seam.

OK, SO NOW YOUR ROOM LOOKS AMAZINGLY COOL, YOU'VE BROUGHT A LITTLE BIT OF STYLE TO YOUR SCHOOL, AND YOUR FRIENDS LOVE ALL THEIR PRESENTS AND THE THINGS THEY MADE WITH YOU. WHAT'S LEFT TO TRANSFORM WITH YOUR CREATIVE TOUCH? WHAT ABOUT YOU?

The projects in this section of the book show you ways to express your style and your totally unique you-ness by wearing it all over! You can make your own jewelry, T-shirts, bags, and accessories, and let the world witness the power of your imagination!

Sure, shopping can be fun, and we all want that perfect new shirt/necklace/pair of jeans every once in a while. But it's so much *more* fun to pick out colors and materials that say YOU, and put together a new look yourself. You'll feel great about what you've accomplished, and you'll get lots of compliments. You may even start getting requests from your friends or even strangers on the street who say, "I want one of those, too!"

Fantasy Flip-Flops

HERE COMES SUMMER! ARE YOUR FEET READY? DON'T SPEND YOUR MONEY ON FANCY FLOPS WHEN YOU CAN MAKE THEM YOURSELF FOR A FRACTION OF THE PRICE. BUY CHEAP FLIP-FLOPS, DRESS 'EM UP, AND EXPRESS YOURSELF. THE ONES SHOWN HERE ARE JUST A FEW OF THE DESIGNS YOU CAN MAKE. LET YOUR IMAGINATION RUN WILD!

GET READY!
~·~·~·~·~·~·~

Flip-flops

TAKE YOUR PICK
~·~·~·~·~·~·~

Silk flowers

Thin-gauge wire

Hot glue gun and glue sticks (optional)

Plastic jewels or rhinestones

Pink Flowery Flip-Flops

Get a bunch (literally) of silk flowers that have two flowers of the same size on a stem. Something big and splashy makes an impact. Cut the flowers off the stem right at the base. Pull the green plastic base off and you'll see a hole. Thread some thin-gauge wire through the hole. Place the flower on the middle of the thong part of the flip-flop and wrap the wire around each side of the thong to secure the flower to the flip-flop. Some flip-flop thongs are thin enough that you can poke the wire right through them. As an alternative, you could hot glue the flower to the thong. Repeat for the other flip-flop, and enjoy your new fashion look!

Blue Jeweled Flip-Flops

Pick out an assortment of plastic jewels or rhinestones—the bigger the better. Hot glue the jewels to the thong part of the flip-flops in the pattern of your choice. Hot glue jewels to the sides on the foamy bottom part of the flip-flops, too. Let the glue dry overnight. Then, go out and have some summer fun in style!

P.S. Cover the surface of your flip- flop with self-stick holographic paper, then seal it with clear self-adhesive shelf paper so it doesn't peel off.

89

I Gotta Be Me!! Tees
Marquee T-shirts

A T-SHIRT IS THE CANVAS YOU CAN USE TO SHOW (AND TELL) THE WORLD JUST WHO YOU ARE. SURE, YOU COULD JUST GO BUY A DECORATED T-SHIRT, BUT WHY LOOK LIKE EVERY OTHER GIRL? HERE ARE A COUPLE OF EASY WAYS TO SHOUT OUT "I GOTTA BE ME!"

GET READY!
~.~.~.~.~.~.~.~

T-shirt

Newspaper

Pencil

Fabric paints or acrylic paints and fabric medium

Small paintbrushes

Paint pens

Dimensional paint

Scissors

Craft foam sheets

White glue

Beads (optional)

Sewing needle and thread (optional)

Hook-and-loop fastener tape with peel-and-stick backing

1. Fold the newspaper to fit inside your T-shirt. It's important to put newspaper inside the shirt so the paint on the front won't soak through to the back!

2. Use the pencil to sketch out the basic shape of the marquee. It can be rectangular, oval, or any shape you wish.

3. Paint the shape with fabric paint, or mix acrylic paint and fabric medium according to the manufacturer's directions. Let the paint dry.

4. You will need at least one more coat (and possibly more) for even coverage. You want your shirt to look nice, don't you? Let the paint dry.

5. Outline the shape with paint and a very small paintbrush, paint pens, or dimensional paints. Let the paint dry.

90

6. Pick a message, saying, or word for your T-shirt. Cut a base shape out of craft foam, and cut letters from a contrasting color of craft foam. Glue the letters to the craft foam shape, and let it dry. Make a couple of different shapes and sayings while you're at it.

7. You can sew or glue beads to the foam base or letters if you wish. Glue on jewels or rhinestones if you're into a glamorous look.

8. Use hook-and-loop tape with peel-and-stick backing to place the foam on the marquee. Put the hook part on the T-shirt and the loop part on your foam base.

What's Your Sign? T-Shirt

JUST SO EVERYONE WILL KNOW YOUR SIGN (NOT TO MENTION YOUR BIRTHDAY, SO YOU DON'T HAVE TO DROP ANY HINTS!), CREATE A ZODIAC T-SHIRT! IF YOU'RE LOOKING FOR A SPECIAL BIRTHDAY PRESENT TO MAKE FOR SOMEONE, THIS IS IT. EACH ASTROLOGICAL SIGN HAS A COLOR ASSOCIATED WITH IT, SO IF YOU REALLY WANT TO GO ALL OUT, CHOOSE YOUR T-SHIRT COLOR TO MATCH THE ZODIAC SIGN!

GET READY!
~.~.~.~.~.~.~.~

T-shirt

Scrap paper

Flat-backed rhinestones or jewels

Sharp pencil or ballpoint pen

Wax paper

Washable glue

1. Find the glyph (symbol) for the astrological sign you're looking for (check the list on pages 94-95).

2. Draw the glyph in the size you want on a piece of scrap paper. Add the birth date if you want.

3. Try spacing the rhinestones on your drawing. If you find you need more, now is the time to find it out, not halfway through the project. When you are happy with the way the rhinestones look, make a small dot next to each one with a pencil. Move the rhinestones to the side.

4. Tear off a length of wax paper to fit inside the T-shirt. This will keep the glue

from seeping onto the back of the T-shirt.

5. Lay your T-shirt on a flat surface. Slip in the wax paper.

6. Lay your drawing on the T-shirt. Use your pencil to prick a hole on the line of the drawing next to where you made a small dot. This will help you keep the spacing just the way you want it. Make sure that the pencil or pen is actually poking through and marking the T-shirt.

7. Put a small dot of glue on each rhinestone and glue them into place. Let the glue dry overnight. Follow the manufacturer's recommendations before washing the jeweled T-shirt.

What's the Word? T-Shirt?

PICK A WORD THAT TELLS EVERYONE YOUR HOBBY, LIKE "DANCE," OR "GOALIE," THEN USE RHINESTONES OR FLAT-BACKED JEWELS TO WRITE THE WORD ON A T-SHIRT.

If you can't decide on a word, how about a symbol, like a star, butterfly, or rainbow?

Follow the instructions for designing and creating the rhinestone glyph T-shirt to write your word or make your symbol on a T-shirt.

To dress up your T-shirt a little more, you can use fabric paint or dimensional paint to add designs to the neckline or the sleeves. Just make sure you put a piece of cardboard inside your T-shirt so that the paint doesn't seep through to the other side.

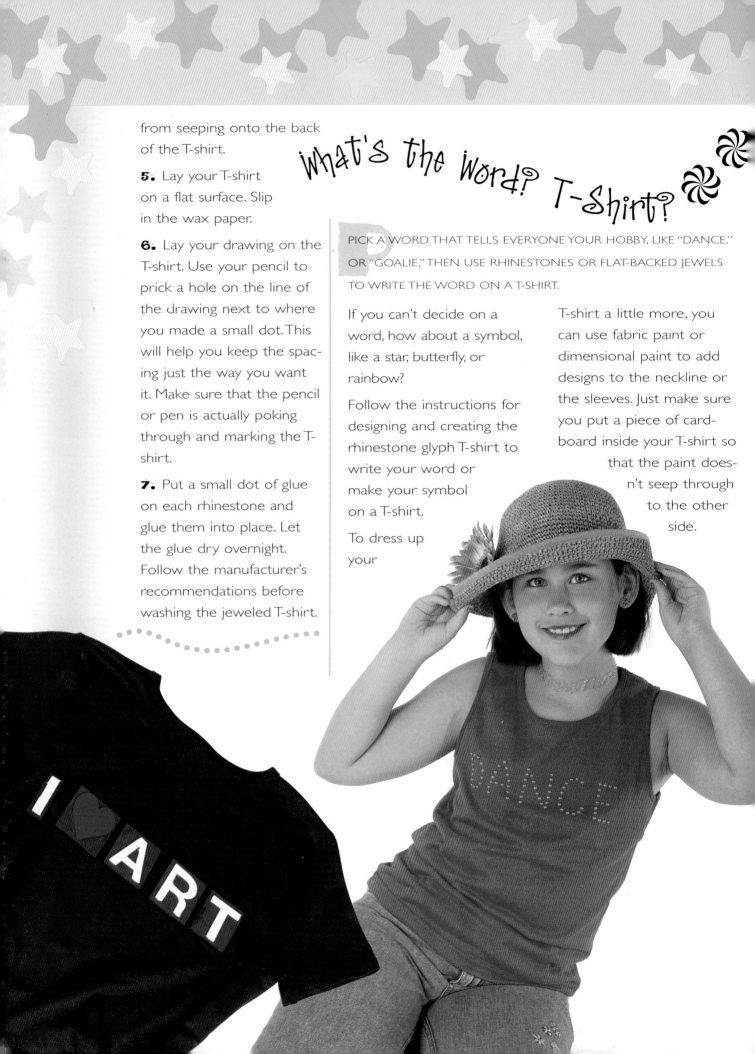

Dreamy Diva Eye Mask

DAHLING, HOW WILL YOU EVER GET YOUR BEAUTY SLEEP WITH THAT LIGHT SHINING IN YOUR EYES? WHAT? YOUR BIG SISTER IS STAYING UP LATE AND WON'T TURN OUT THE LIGHT SO YOU CAN CATCH YOUR ZZZS? SLIP ON THIS GLAMOROUS EYE MASK, ROLL OVER, AND DRIFT INTO A PEACEFUL SLEEP.

GET READY!

Fabric eye mask

Small plastic jewels

Dimensional paint

1. Make small dots of dimensional paint evenly spaced around the edge of the eye mask.

2. Place one jewel in the center of each dot.

3. Trace around the edges of each jewel with the dimensional paint, and connect the spaces between the jewels with paint. Make small dots with the paint between every jewel.

93

WHAT'S YOUR SIGN?

You may know your zodiac sign, but do you know its symbol? Each zodiac sign has a symbol, called a glyph, that represents it. The zodiac signs get their names from the constellations, which got their names from ancient Greek mythology. In addition to a glyph, each zodiac sign is associated with a color, a gemstone, and a flower. Read about your sign and its symbols in the following chart. You can also do more research at your library or on the Internet. Look up your daily horoscope in the newspaper to see if sounds like you!

ZODIAC SYMBOLS

ARIES

March 21 to April 20

The Ram

Color: Red

Gemstone: Ruby

Flower: Rose

The symbol represents a magical ram who helped the son of a king. According to the myth, Zeus (the king of the Gods) placed the ram in the sky as a reward. The ram is the same ram with the golden fleece that Jason and the Argonauts went searching for in that famous myth. Aries people are said to be generous and brave, but can have bad tempers.

TAURUS

April 21 to May 20

The Bull

Color: Blue

Gemstone: Sapphire

Flower: Lily of the Valley

The bull represents Zeus, the king of the gods. In one story, Zeus, who liked tricking humans, became a bull so that he could run away with Europa, a beautiful woman. Taureans are athletic and fair-minded, but stubborn.

GEMINI

May 21 to June 21

The Twins

Colors: White and Silver

Gemstone: Diamond

Flower: Snapdragon

The Gemini sign represents the twins Castor and Pollux. Their mother was human, but their father was Zeus. There are different stories about how they died, but the ancient Greeks believed that Zeus placed them in the sky after their death. Geminis are friendly, free-spirited, creative, and a little unreliable.

CANCER

June 22 to July 22

The Crab

Color: Green

Gemstone: Emerald

Flower: Poppy

The Cancer crab comes to us from the myth of Heracles, a hero, and his fight with the hydra, a monster. While he was fighting the monster, a crab pinched him. Even though he was the good guy, he had made enemies with Hera, the queen of the gods. Hera put the crab in the sky as a reward for pinching Heracles. Cancers are said to be creative, sensitive, and helpful.

LEO

July 23 to August 22

The Lion

Color: Gold

Gemstones: Amber and Topaz

Flowers: Marigold or Sunflower

The Leo lion comes from the story of Heracles (again). This time, Heracles won and the lion was put in the sky. Leos are known as good leaders. They are brave and friendly, but sometimes bossy.

VIRGO

August 23 to September 22

The Virgin

Color: Yellow

Gemstone: Jade

Flower: Valerian

The Virgo symbolizes Persephone, the goddess of the harvest. The squiggles on the right side represent wheat, which was a big part of the harvest. Virgos are dependable, hard-working, and honest, but they can be picky.

LIBRA

September 22 to October 23

The Scales

Color: Violet

Gemstone: Opal

Flower: Violet

The symbol represents a woman holding the scales of justice (an instrument that symbolizes weighing facts to come to a just conclusion). The woman who is often seen with the scales may be Astraea, the Roman goddess of justice. Libras are kind and fair-minded, but can have a hard time making decisions.

SCORPIO

October 24 to November 21

The Scorpion

Color: Red

Gemstone: Ruby

Flower: Chrysanthemum

Orion was another famous hero in mythology. He was stung to death by a scorpion, who, again, was placed in the sky by Zeus.

Scorpios are creative and mysterious, but can be hurtful and jealous.

SAGITTARIUS

November 22 to December 21

The Archer

Color: Orange

Gemstone: Sapphire

Flower: Carnation

The archer is a centaur (ancient mythological creature) with a bow and arrow. There's no particular story about this particular centaur; they were just common in Greek mythology. Saggitarians are curious and friendly, but can be a bit insensitive.

CAPRICORN

December 22 to January 19

The Goat

Color: Black

Gemstone: Onyx

Flower: Nightshade

The Capricorn symbol represents Pan, a god of the forest. He was half man and half goat. According to myth, he was being chased and jumped in the water and became half-goat, half-fish. The Capricorn glyph represents his head sticking up from under the water. Capricorns are mature, respectful, and organized, but a little shy.

AQUARIUS

January 20 to February 18

The Water Bearer

Color: Blue

Gemstone: Garnet

Flower: Foxglove

The symbol is a person holding two big jugs of water and pouring them out. No one's really sure why, but some people think it represents the rainy season in ancient Greece. Aquarians are deep thinkers, love nature, and are a little rebellious.

PISCES

February 19 to March 20

The Fish

Color: Purple

Gemstone: Aquamarine

Flower: Carnation

The symbol is two fish tied together. They represent Aphrodite (the goddess of love) and Eros (her son). Legend has it that they were being chased by a monster, so they jumped into a river and turned into fish (sound familiar?). Pisceans are artistic, creative, and don't like routines.

Cuff Stuff 🌀 🌀

CUFFS ARE COOL! YOU CAN SEE THEM IN LOTS OF FASHION MAGAZINES AND CATALOGUES, SELLING FOR BIG BUCKS. SAVE YOUR CASH FOR SOMETHING ELSE AND DESIGN YOUR OWN CUFFS TO SUIT YOUR STYLE! ALL YOU NEED TO GET STARTED IS A GREAT IMAGINATION, CRAFT FOAM, AND YOUR FAVORITE MATERIALS FROM FABRIC AND CRAFT STORES. MAKE ONE FOR YOUR FRIEND OR SISTER, TOO! ONE CUFF IS NOT ENOUGH!

GET READY!
~.~.~.~.~.~.~

Cloth measuring tape

Craft foam

Pencil

Scissors

Hot glue gun and glue sticks

TAKE YOUR PICK
~.~.~.~.~.~.~

Ribbon

Small hook-and-loop fastener tape with peel-and-stick backing

Sequins, buttons, or beads

Sewing needle and thread

1. First you'll need to measure your wrist to see how long and wide your cuff will need to be. Measure around your wrist with a cloth measuring tape. Add about 1 inch (2.5 cm) to that measurement, and mark it on your foam sheet. Hold the sheet up to your wrist and decide how wide you want your cuff to be. Mark the width on the cuff and cut it. Re-check the fit and cut off any excess length. You should have a little overlap at the ends rather than having each end butt up against the other.

2. The width of your ribbon should be narrower than the width of your cuff. The ribbon's length should be the same length as the cuff. Hold the ribbon next to the cuff and cut the ribbon to the correct size.

3. Center the ribbon on your cuff. Apply a small

Hair Flair!

amount of hot glue to one edge of the cuff, and press the ribbon in place. Work your way down the length of the cuff, hot gluing and pressing down the ribbon a little at a time until you've covered the whole cuff. Allow the glue to cool completely and dry. Re-glue any loose edges.

4. Attach one loop piece of hook-and-loop tape, and press it near one end on the front of the cuff. Turn the cuff over and adhere a hook piece on the back of the opposite side of the cuff. To be extra sure they'll stick, you may want to hot glue them into position.

5. Choose sequins, buttons, or beads to decorate your cuff. Experiment with the design for your cuff, moving the beads, sequins, buttons, etc., around until you love the look. Hot glue the decorations in place, or use a needle and thread to sew on buttons and beads. Let everything dry and settle on a flat surface overnight before wearing your cuff.

UNTIL YOU WERE ABOUT THREE YEARS OLD, YOU PROBABLY HAD ONE HAIRSTYLE AND ONE ONLY: A LITTLE SPOUT OF HAIR RIGHT ON TOP OF YOUR HEAD LIKE A FOUNTAIN. AREN'T YOU GLAD YOU HAVE MORE CHOICES (AND MORE HAIR) NOW? YOU CAN PICK A DIFFERENT STYLE FOR EVERY DAY OF THE WEEK, AND MAKE YOUR OWN COMPLETELY ORIGINAL HAIR ACCESSORIES TO SUIT YOUR STYLE—A BRIGHT BEADED HAIR ELASTIC, A ROMANTIC RIBBON ROSE, OR A SPARKLY METAL CLIP. THEY'RE ALL SO EASY. YOU'LL SPEND MORE TIME PICKING OUT YOUR MATERIALS THAN YOU WILL MAKING THEM!

GET READY!
~.~.~.~.~.~.~.~

Hair elastics in different colors

Metal barrettes

Metal hair clips

Bobby pins

TAKE YOUR PICK
~.~.~.~.~.~.~.~

Beads

24-gauge wire (test to see if a double strand of wire will slip through the beads)

Wire cutters

Pliers

Scissors

Hot glue gun and glue sticks

Silk flowers

Feather boa

Thin ribbon

Medium-sized ribbons

Sewing needle and thread

Thread

Nail polish (clear, colored, and glitter)

Glitter

Epoxy

Rhinestones

Beads

Beaded Hair Elastics

Thread beads onto a small piece of 16-gauge wire. Wrap one end of the wire tightly around the elastic.  Wrap the beaded wire around the elastic four times, then finish with a figure-eight (see the illustration above). Secure the end of the wire by twisting it under another part of the wire. Cut off the excess wire with the wire cutters.

Silk Flower Hair Elastics

Clip the silk flowers off their stems at the base with wire cutters. Attach the flower to the elastic with hot glue. If you want, cover the base with silk leaves.

Ribbon Barrettes

Use double bar clips and two different colored ribbons, each about 18 inches (45.7 cm). Start at one end, open the clip, and wrap the ribbon around the base. Start weaving the ribbon through the clip in a criss-cross pattern (see the illustration above). 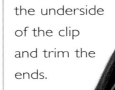 When the clip is completely covered, tie the ribbon in a knot on the underside of the clip and trim the ends.

Glittery Clips

Paint the plain, cheap clips you get at any drug store with nail polish. You can pick a solid color, then paint over it with glitter nail polish. Or you can paint your clip a solid color, dab epoxy on top of it, then put it in a paper bag full of glitter and shake it. When you take it out, it will be covered in glitter. When the glitter has set, paint it with clear nail polish to seal it. Or you can paint your clip a solid color, paint little flowers or stars on it, and then seal it with clear nail polish.

Boa Hair Elastics

Cut a 2-inch (5.1 cm) piece from a boa and attach it to your hair elastic with hot glue. Seal the ends with hot glue so they don't unravel.

Ribbon Rosebud Hair Elastics

You can make these with different types of ribbon. These were made with hand-dyed silk ribbon.

1. Fold over one edge of your ribbon at a 90° angle.

2. Begin rolling the ribbon at the right bottom point, forming a tag to hold onto.

3. Roll the ribbon as shown in the illustration, left.

4. Fold back the ribbon at a 90° angle.

5. Roll again to the other edge, so that the outer petal flares slightly (see illustration, right).

6. Tuck in the end of the ribbon and sew it at the bottom with three or four stitches on top of each other. Make a knot and cut the excess thread.

Beaded Bobby Pins

1. Make a skinny U shape with the wire.

2. Slip the wire under the straight side of the pin. Slide the U shape up to the bend in the bobby pin. Twist the wire tightly to the bobby pin a few times to hold it in place. Both sides of the folded wire should be outside the bobby pin.

3. Hold the two sides of the wire together and slide on a small bead, threading both sides of the wire through its hole. Next, slide on your big heart or other special bead in the same way. Continue sliding the beads onto the wires until you've threaded on enough to reach the end of the bobby pin.

4. Holding the bobby pin in one hand and the wire in the other, start wrapping each side of the wire around the end of the bobby pin, near the rubber tip. Once you've wrapped the wires around enough to secure the beaded wire, start wrapping the excess wire diagonally back up the bobby pin, slipping the wire between beads as you wind it. Wind up one wire, then the other.

5. When you get back up to the big heart or other special bead, wrap the wires under the bottom of the bead. Wrap your wires tightly around the pin one more time. Cut the ends as close to the pin as you can. If there is a little piece sticking up, poke it down between beads.

Twisted Beaded Bobby Pins

1. Follow steps 1 and 2 for the regular beaded bobby pins. Then, instead of threading your beads through the two wires at once, you will thread beads onto each strand of the wire. Thread beads onto each strand almost down to the tip of the pin.

2. Twist the two wires together at the end of the beads to secure the beads. Then twist the beaded wires together loosely.

3. Wind the wires together around the end of the pin. Separate the strands and wind each one diagonally back up towards the bend. This will secure the twisted beads to the pin. Wind tightly at the top and trim off the excess wire.

La Boa Hem!!

SO YOU'RE ALREADY TIRED OF THE SKIRT THAT YOU **HAD TO** HAVE LAST SEASON? DON'T THROW IT AWAY! ADD A BOA TO THE HEM AND YOU'LL FALL IN LOVE WITH IT ALL OVER AGAIN. WITH THIS QUICK MAKEOVER, YOU'LL ADD INSTANT GLAMOUR TO YOUR WARDROBE, AND YOU'LL ENJOY THAT FEATHERY LITTLE TICKLE AROUND YOUR KNEES!

GET READY!
~.~.~.~.~.~.~.~

Skirt

Feathered boa, twice as long as the skirt's bottom, plus about 3 inches (7.6 cm) extra

Straight pins or safety pins

Scissors

Sewing needle and thread

1. Begin by pinning the feathered boa to the bottom edge of the skirt. You may need to use safety pins to hold it firmly in place. Don't cut your boa yet, just in case you need extra when you get all the way around the skirt.

2. Cut a long length of thread, feed it through the needle, and knot it at the end. Pull the needle and thread through the bottom of the skirt at the side seam, moving from the inside of the skirt to the outside.

3. Pull the needle and thread over the feathered boa and back through to the inside of the skirt. Continue sewing the boa to the skirt this way, making a stitch every ¼ inch (6 mm) or so.

4. Once you have sewn the entire boa to the skirt, stitch the thread over your last stitch several times and knot it. You want to make sure the end is secure. Now cut off the remaining end of the boa.

Pick-A-Flower Necklace

LOOKING FOR THE PERFECT NECKLACE TO GO WITH YOUR PARTY DRESS, YOUR SCHOOL CLOTHES, AND YOUR JEANS? LOOK NO FURTHER THAN YOUR LOCAL CRAFT STORE. GET SOME COOL RIBBON AND A VARIETY OF SILK FLOWERS TO MATCH DIFFERENT OUT-FITS. PUT THEM TOGETHER AND YOU'VE GOT AN INTER-CHANGEABLE FLOWER NECK-LACE THAT YOU DESIGN YOUR-SELF!

GET READY!
~.~.~.~.~.~.~.~

Ribbon (enough to fit around your neck)

Hot glue gun and glue sticks

Hook-and-loop tape with peel-and-stick backing

Permanent marker

Silk flowers

1. Fit the ribbon to your neck to see how long a piece you need. Measure out about 2 inches (5.1 cm) extra just in case, then cut the ribbon.

2. Fold back about ½ inch (1.3 cm) on each end of the ribbon. Apply a small dot of hot glue to the fold-ed part to attach it to the back of the ribbon. It will make a small tab. Let the glue cool and set for 30 minutes.

3. Put a small piece of hook-and-loop tape on each tab at the end of the ribbon (one side gets a hook and the other gets a loop).

4. Fit the ribbon to your neck again to see where the center of your neck is on the ribbon. Mark the spot with a permanent marker. Hot glue a small hook piece of tape on top of the mark.

5. Cut a flower off its stem, and hot glue a loop piece of tape onto the base.

6. Attach the flower to your necklace and wear it! Change the silk flowers to match whatever outfit you want.

Groovy Girl Bandana

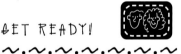

B BANDANAS ARE VERY VERSA-
TILE. YOU CAN USE THEM ON
YOUR HEAD TO HOLD BACK
YOUR HAIR OR ACCESSORIZE
YOUR OUTFIT. YOU CAN TWIST
THEM UP AND USE THEM
AROUND YOUR WAIST AS A
BELT. SOME PEOPLE EVEN PUT
THEM ON THEIR DOGS! WITH
SO MANY USES, DON'T YOU
THINK YOU SHOULD HAVE A
FEW BANDANAS IN YOUR
WARDROBE? START YOUR
COLLECTION WITH AN EASY-
TO-MAKE ONE IN GROOVY
FABRIC. ONCE YOU KNOW
HOW, YOU CAN MAKE A MIL-
LION MORE AND GIVE THEM
AS GIFTS!

GET READY!
~·~·~·~·~·~·~·~

½ yard (45.7 cm) of groovy
material

Chalk (or pencil)

Ruler

Pinking shears

Iron

18 inches (45.7 cm) of
matching ribbon

Straight pins

Sewing needle and thread

Thread

1. Draw an 18-inch (45.7
cm) square on your fabric
with chalk or a pencil.

2. Cut out the square with
the pinking shears.

3. Fold the square (back
sides together) to make a
triangle with two short
sides and one longer side.
Have an adult iron the fabric for you so it stays
together in the triangle
shape.

4. Cut your
ribbon in
half.

5. Pin 3 inches (7.6 cm) of
one piece of ribbon to one
end of the longer side of
the triangle. Pin 3 inches
(7.6 cm) of the other piece
of ribbon to the opposite
end of the longer side of
the triangle.

6. Use the needle and
thread to sew the ribbon
onto the fabric, and then
remove the pins.

Blue Jeans Forever! Shoulder Bag

ARE YOU HAVING TROUBLE PARTING WITH YOUR FAVORITE PAIR OF JEANS EVEN THOUGH YOU OUTGREW THEM MONTHS AGO? DON'T WORRY—MAKE A SHOULDER BAG OUT OF THEM AND YOU'LL NEVER HAVE TO SAY GOOD-BYE! THE SEWING FOR THIS BAG IS SO SIMPLE, YOU'LL BE DONE IN TIME TO WEAR IT TO SCHOOL TOMORROW. THEN YOU CAN ADD ON BEADS, BUTTONS, AND IRON-ON PATCHES, OR WRITE ON YOUR BAG WITH PERMANENT MARKERS. YOUR JEANS BAG WILL KEEP GOING LONG AFTER YOUR FAVORITE SHOES HAVE WORN OUT!

GET READY!

Old pair of jeans

Scissors

Sewing needle and thread

Embroidery floss ☞

2 yards (1.8 m) of wide ribbon

Permanent markers

Beads, buttons, and embellishments of your choice

☞ This is a sturdy kind of thread for heavy-duty stitching.

1. Wash your old jeans and cut them off 1½ inches (3.8 cm) below the crotch.

2. Turn the jeans inside out, and sew the legs closed with a backstitch (see page 12).

3. Turn the jeans right side out. Create the strap by sewing the wide ribbon on the inside of the jeans, one side on each hip.

4. Decorate your bag any way you want. You can embroider flowers, draw, make hearts, do beadwork, and just keep adding to it whenever the mood hits you!

Fashion Passion Foam Belts

LET'S FACE IT: FASHION IS FLEETING. YOU MAY HAVE THE PERFECT ACCESSORY THIS MONTH, ONLY TO FIND OUT THAT NEXT MONTH IT'S SOOO 15 MINUTES AGO. TO KEEP UP WITH THE BRISK PACE OF FASHION WITHOUT SPENDING NEXT MONTH'S ALLOWANCE, MAKE YOUR OWN BELTS FROM CRAFT FOAM—IT TAKES ONLY A FEW MINUTES TO MAKE. DECORATE YOUR BELT WITH HOLO-GRAPHIC PAPER, RIBBON, RHINESTONES, STUDS—WHAT-EVER SAYS "YOU." BUCKLE UP AND SHOW OFF YOUR STYLE!

Dancing Queen Belt

GET READY!
~.~.~.~.~.~.~.~

Plastic belt buckle 🐱

Spray paint (silver and glitter)

Clear nail polish

Tape measure

Black craft foam sheet

Scissors

Hot glue gun and glue sticks

Heavy weight (a big diction-ary works)

Holographic paper with peel-and-stick backing

Stapler and staples (optional)

🐱 fabric store

1. Spray paint your belt buckle sparkling silver. You'll probably need to use a few coats to get it to stick. When the paint dries (about 1 hour), seal it with clear nail polish.

2. Measure your waist with a tape measure, then measure the open-ing of your belt buckle.

3. Since foam sheets are usually fairly short, you'll proba-bly need two strips to go around your waist. Cut each strip so the length of both pieces combined is about 6 inches (15.2 cm) longer than your waist measurement.

The width of the strip must fit snuggly inside the belt buckle.

4. Hot glue the strips together to make one long strip. Put a heavy weight (such as a big dictionary) on top of the strip, and let it set overnight.

5. Thread the belt through the belt buckles, folding a few inches of the belt back inside the buckles. Fit it to your waist to figure out how much you need to cut off the belt.

6. Cut off the excess belt, leaving at least 2 inches

(5.1 cm) folded back behind the buckle.

7. Hot glue the folded overlap part to the back of the belt. Don't touch the tip of the glue gun to the foam—it may melt it. To make sure the bond is secure, try stapling it, too. Staple from the back to the front and the staple won't show through on the front of your belt.

8. Cut small pieces of holographic paper the same width as the belt. Lay the belt flat to figure out how many pieces of paper you'll need to decorate it. Experiment with the placement of the paper before adhering it to the belt.

9. Once you've decided on a design, peel the backing off the

holographic paper and stick the paper to the belt at equal intervals. Now, go and dance the night away!

Preppy Belt

GET READY!
~.~.~.~.~.~.~

Plastic belt buckle

Craft foam sheet

2 yards (1.8 m) of rainbow ribbon

Scissors

Measuring tape

Craft glue (clear-drying)

1. Follow steps 2 through 6 for the Dancing Queen belt.

2. Since the belt buckle used for this belt only has one piece, you only need to thread each piece of the belt through the center of the buckle. Your overlapping part will go behind the other side of the belt.

3. Once the belt is the size you want, measure the ribbon to 2 inches (5.1 cm) longer than the length of your belt, and cut it.

4. Apply clear-drying glue evenly to one side of the ribbon. Center it and lay it down on the belt. Fold the ends of the ribbon over the back of the belt and press it in place. Make sure the glue doesn't clump or streak because it may show through on the ribbon. Cut away any excess ribbon. Let the belt and the ribbon bond overnight.

5. Thread the belt through the belt buckle, and enjoy your new look!

Say It With Flowers Pouch

EVERY GIRL HAS AT LEAST TWO SIDES. SOMETIMES YOU WANT TO WEAR A T-SHIRT AND JEANS. SOMETIMES YOU WANT TO WEAR SOMETHING A LITTLE MORE DRESSY. FOR THOSE MOMENTS, THIS IS YOUR PURSE. IT'S PERFECT FOR SPECIAL OCCASIONS—PICK ANY FLOWERS YOU LIKE TO MATCH THE FABRIC OF YOUR BAG AND THE FEEL OF YOUR OUTFIT. WE USED DAISIES, BUT YOU COULD TRY FANCY ROSES, SPLASHY HIBISCUS, OR EVEN A MIXED BOUQUET!

GET READY!

1 yard (91.4 cm) blue fabric

Pencil

Measuring tape

Scissors

Sewing needle and thread

Iron

Seam gauge ☛

20 to 25 silk daisies

Hot glue gun and glue sticks

2 yards (1.8 m) satin cording

Safety pin

☛ This is a little instrument that you can use to make sure you're sewing a straight line. You can get one in a fabric store, and it's usually very cheap.

DO-IT-YOURSELF DABBLER WAY

Buy a pouch. Hot glue the silk flowers of your choice to your pouch.

CRAFT QUEEN WAY

1. Fold the fabric in half. Find the center point of the fabric and mark it lightly with a pencil. Unfold the fabric and measure out from this center point 14 inches (35.6 cm) in all directions, making a light pencil mark each time. Connect the dots to make a large circle. Cut out the circle.

FIGURE 1

FIGURE 2

106

2. Fold the circle in half. Measure 3 inches (7.6 cm) in from the edge of the fold on each side, and make a mark. You only need to do this on one side of the folded fabric, not both. The marks will indicate where your buttonholes will be (see Figure 1).

3. Unfold the fabric, and make buttonholes with scissors in the place where you made your mark in step 2.

4. Fold your fabric again, with the printed sides facing in. Sew the two sides together ½ inch (1.3 cm) in from the edge. Leave a 2-inch (5.1 cm) opening so you can turn your fabric right side out when you're done.

5. Turn the fabric right side out and press it with an iron. Stitch the opening closed.

6. Using the seam gauge to mark your position, sew a circle 2 inches (5.1 cm) in from the outer edge. Don't sew across the buttonholes. Sew a second circle 3 inches (7.6 cm) in from the outer edge. This will make a 1-inch (2.5 cm) pocket for you to thread your cord through.

7. Hot glue your flowers to the bag (below the cord pocket).

8. Cut the satin cord in half. Tape the cord's ends so they don't unravel. Attach a safety pin to the end of one cord, and use it to thread the cord into the buttonhole and through the narrow cord pocket. Make sure the cord goes in and out of the same buttonhole. Tie the ends together and remove the tape. Repeat the process with the other half of the cord and the other buttonhole (see Figure 2).

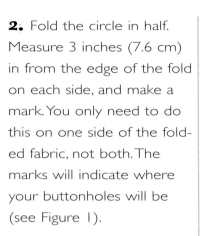

107

Bracelets Beaucoup!!

Pins Are In!! Safety Pin Bracelet

MA CHÈRIE (THAT'S FRENCH FOR "MY DEAR"), DID YOU KNOW THAT THE FRENCH WORD FOR BRACELET IS *BRACELET*? OF COURSE, IN FRENCH IT'S PRONOUNCED DIFFERENTLY (BRAH-CE-LET), BUT IF YOU EVER GO TO FRANCE, AT LEAST YOU WILL KNOW WHAT PEOPLE ARE SAYING WHEN THEY SAY "MA CHÈRIE, TON BRACELET EST TRES JOLI!" ("MY DEAR, YOUR BRACELET IS VERY PRETTY!"). HERE ARE BEAUCOUP (A LOT OF) DIFFERENT BEAUTIFUL BRACELETS TO MAKE THAT WILL DAZZLE IN ANY LANGUAGE.

(IN THE PHOTO ABOVE, THE BRACELETS ON THE FIRST AND THIRD HANDS ARE FROM PAGE 72)

GET READY!
~·~·~·~·~·~·~

35 to 50 safety pins

Bugle beads

Seed beads

Scissors

2 pieces of elastic cord

Tape

E beads (large beads) or spacers

Cloth measuring tape

Clear nail polish

1. Open up a safety pin. Thread as many seed beads and bugle beads as you can onto the pin in any pattern you like, then close the pin. Repeat this process for as many

safety pins as you have.

2. Measure your wrist and add ¾ inch (1.9 cm). This is how long your bracelet should be. Cut your elastic to this size.

3. Tape one end of the elastic cord to a worktable.

4. Poke the free end of the elastic cord through the round hole at the bottom of a pin, and thread on an E bead.

5. Thread on another pin and another E bead.

6. Repeat steps 4 and 5 until you reach the last ¾ inch (1.9 cm) of elastic, and end with an E bead.

7. Untape the elastic and tie its two ends together.

8. Repeat the process for the other elastic cord. Tape it to your worktable, run it

through the free end of the pins, and thread it the way it's done in steps 4 through 6. Tie the ends together.

9. Trim the ends of your elastic and dab a little clear nail polish on them to keep the knot from opening up.

Button it Up! Bracelet

GET READY!
~.~.~.~.~.~.~

Cloth measuring tape

Elastic trim

Thread

Needle

Scissors

Buttons and beads 🐱 🐱

🐱 fabric store

🐱 🐱 Yard sales and second-hand stores are great places to find vintage buttons.

1. Measure elastic to fit around your wrist, and cut it. Sew the ends together.

2. Select buttons and

beads. Sew them to the elastic (poking through from the inside to the outside) until you can barely see the elastic under all the buttons.

Sparkle-on-a-String Bracelet

GET READY!
~.~.~.~.~.~.~

Elastic cord

Scissors

Measuring tape or ruler

Tape

Sequins 🐱

Small beads

Medium-sized beads

Craft glue (optional)

Clear nail polish (optional)

🐱 craft and fabric stores

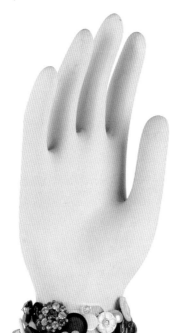

1. Take the elastic cord and wrap it loosely around your wrist. Cut the elastic about 3 inches (7.6 cm) longer than the circumference of your wrist (this will leave

you room to make mistakes and to tie a knot at the end).

2. Stick a small piece of tape on one end of the

elastic cord and fold it over onto itself. This will keep the sequins from sliding off the end of the cord while you're stringing them—a frustrating (and messy) experience!

3. Begin stringing the sequins onto the elastic cord. If the surfaces of your sequins are slightly curved, make sure you string the sequins so they all face the same direction.

4. You don't need to count the exact number of sequins between each set

of beads; just string on about ¾ inch (1.9 cm) of sequins, then add a small bead, a medium-size bead, and another small bead. Continue adding sequins and beads until you have about 3 inches (7.6 cm) of elastic cord left.

5. After you've strung on the last sequin or bead, place another piece of tape on the cord, and then wrap the bracelet around your wrist to test for size (the bracelet should not be too tight). Once you've tested for size, remove the piece of tape, and add or remove sequins and beads as need-ed. Remember, since you started the pattern with sequins, you'll want to end with beads.

6. Once you've added beads and sequins to the correct point on your cord, remove the tape from the beginning of the bracelet and carefully tie the elastic cord in a knot that fits tight up against the sequins or beads on either side. It's a good idea to add a drop of glue or clear nail polish to the knot to keep it from coming undone.

Safari Shoulder Ba

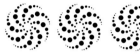

IT'S A JUNGLE OUT THERE,
BE PREPARED. STEP OUT IN
STYLE WITH A SWINGIN'
SAFARI SHOULDER BAG TH
CAN CARRY ALL YOUR IMP
TANT SUPPLIES. ALL YOU N
TO START WITH IS AN HO
GREAT PIECE OF FABRIC, A
BON, AND SOME BEADED
FRINGE. DON'T BE AFRAID
SEW! THIS IS VERY EASY TO
MAKE, EVEN IF YOU'VE NEV
SEWN ANYTHING BEFORE.
YOU REALLY, REALLY DON'
WANT TO SEW, YOU CAN U
HOT GLUE INSTEAD.

GET READY!
~.~.~.~.~.~.~.

Ruler or measuring tape

Scissors

2 pieces of animal print
fabric in 8-inch (20.3 cm
squares

Straight pins

Sewing thread (get a col
that matches your fabric

Sewing needle

Pencil

Wide decorative ribbon, 36 inches (91.4 cm) long

Ribbon with beaded fringe, 15 inches (38.1 cm) long

 craft stores

NOTE: If you don't want to sew the bag, you can use hot glue along all the edges that require stitching. This includes the seams of the bag, the ribbon handle, and the beaded fringe along the bottom.

1. Measure and cut your fabric. Place the two 8-inch (20.3 cm) squares together, print side facing in. Place several pins through the fabric along three of the edges. This holds the fabric together as you sew.

2. Guide the edge of the thread through the needle, and tie a knot.

3. Pull the needle and thread through a corner of the fabric, approximately ¼ inch (6 mm) in from the edge. Continue sewing through the fabric with a running stitch, keeping the thread ¼ inch (6 mm) from the edge at all times. You may want to draw a straight line with a pencil ¼

inch (6 mm) from the edge to guide you as you sew. Sew like this along the three edges of fabric, taking out the pins as you go. When you reach the end of the third side, tie a strong knot at the end of the stitching. Cut off any excess thread.

4. Leaving the two sewn squares with the print side in, fold over ½ inch (1.3 cm) of fabric along the unsewn top edge of the bag. Pin this flap down, knot more thread, and sew along the edge in a running stitch like you did in step 3. When you reach the end, tie a knot and cut off the excess thread.

5. Decide on the length of your shoulder strap. You can do this by pinning the ribbon to the top of the bag and trying it on to see where the bag falls when you wear it. When you've got the right length, cut the ribbon about 1 inch (2.5 cm) longer than you want it to be. Fold over ½ inch (1.3 cm) at one end of the ribbon. Pin this end inside one side of the bag, centering it over the seam. Sew across the ribbon two times and tie it off with a

knot (see Figure 1). Repeat this step with the other end of the ribbon. Make sure the ribbon is not twisted before you start sewing, and make sure both ends of the ribbon are sewn directly across from each other so that your strap will fall evenly.

6. Turn the bag completely right side out.

7. Take one edge of the beaded fringe ribbon, and place it along the bottom edge of the finished bag. Pin the entire length of the ribbon along the bottom edge. Using a running stitch, sew along the center of the ribbon until the entire bottom is covered. Be sure to take out the pins as you sew. Knot the thread and cut off the excess. Congratulate yourself on making this fabulous fashion accessory!

FIGURE 1

111

INDEX

112

WE GET BY WITH A LITTLE HELP FROM OUR FRIENDS....

Working on a cool project like this book is much more fun when you can do it with friends. Each person brings special talents and lots of great ideas. Joanne and Dana send many thanks to all the people who helped create *Girls' World!*

CREATIVE GENIUS!

Who made all this cool stuff? A *bunch* of creative dynamos who love nothing more than to sit down at a table with a *bunch* of materials and put their great imaginations to work! Kudos and muchos gracias to all our designers! They are professional, enthusiastic, and oh-so-talented!

Theresé de la Baton Rouge (12, 21, 23-24, 34, 35, 50-51, 66, 82, 90-91)

Jennifer Hamilton (16, 18, 25, 28-29, 56, 92, 101)

Dana Irwin (75, and all the cool page designs!)

Marthe Le Van (97)

Corrine Kurzmann (79-80, 99, 103, 108-109)

Leah Sandbach (77-78)

Kathy Sheldon (20, 44-45, 71-72, 83-84, 85-86, 87, 102, 109)

Allison Smith (16, 22, 26, 30-31, 32, 33, 36-37, 48-49, 55-56, 63-64, 68, 69, 71-72, 73-74, 93, 97-99, 106-107)

Nicole Tuggle (53, 54-55, 58-59, 11, 110-11)

Thanks also to Sandra Stambaugh for her most excellent photography, her patience, and her girl power! Mille grazie, Sandra!

A BIG THANK YOU TO OUR MARVELOUS MODELS:

Monique Bowie

Maggie Mathena

Corrina Matthews

Lindsey O'Sullivan

Cece Thomas

Jasmine Villareal

Karla Weiss

Sara Yoeun

And of course, our pet models:

Haywood the Dog

Violet the Kitten

We had a lot of fun working with all our models, and they helped to make the book look great!

Thanks to all the girls who helped us with their input: Stephanie Ariza, Caitlyn Caskey, Lily Cole-Chu, Jessica Butler Daniels, Brittany Ko, Andrea Macias, Yessina Levette Morales, Brooke Pachino, Brenda Lee Reyes, Claire Solomon, Sarah Sperry, Sage Sullivan, Rachael Warriner, and Pamela and Alana, who sent us fun information, but no last names!